Android 15 Programming for Beginners

Step-by-Step Mobile App Development with Kotlin, code samples and Jetpack

Beth Thompson

TABLE OF CONTENTS

Introduction to Android Development

So, you've decided to take your first steps into the world of Android development. Welcome aboard! This world is full of possibilities—from building simple apps that help people track their daily habits, to creating groundbreaking innovations that live in the pockets of millions. If you're curious, creative, and excited about tech that touches everyday life, you're in the right place. Let's start by understanding the foundation of Android and what makes it such a powerful platform in 2025.

What is Android?

Android is an open-source operating system designed primarily for mobile devices like smartphones, tablets, smartwatches, and even TVs and cars. It was originally developed by Android Inc., which was later acquired by Google in 2005. The first commercial version of Android was released in 2008, and since then, it has taken the world by storm.

At its core, Android is based on the Linux kernel and designed to be highly customizable. It gives developers the tools to build applications in the Java and Kotlin programming languages (though Kotlin is now the preferred language).

Android powers billions of devices globally, and it's one of the most accessible ways to reach a massive audience with your ideas.

What makes Android unique is its flexibility. You can design apps that look and feel exactly how you want, and that integrate with almost every piece of a user's digital life—location, camera, sensors, contacts, notifications, voice commands, and more. It's not just a phone OS anymore. It's an ecosystem, and as a developer, you're about to become part of that ecosystem.

What's New in Android 15

Android 15, codenamed "Vanilla Ice Cream," continues to push the boundaries of innovation while focusing on privacy, performance, and personalization. If you're learning Android development today, this is the most powerful version ever—and the best time to start.

Here are some key highlights in Android 15

Dynamic performance profiles
Developers now have better control over how apps behave based on the current system performance mode. Whether a user is in battery-saver mode or high-performance mode, you can tailor your app's experience accordingly.

Improved large-screen and foldable support
Android 15 enhances the experience on tablets and foldables, making it easier than ever to build adaptive layouts that just work across different form factors.

Partial screen sharing

Apps can now support partial screen capture, such as just sharing a single app window during screen recording or casting, giving users more control over their privacy.

Predictive back navigation

Now fully integrated, predictive back navigation offers smoother transitions and clearer context to users when they navigate backwards through your app.

Private space

Users can create a private, locked-down space on their device to store sensitive apps. As a developer, this means you should be aware of where and how users might store your app if it involves privacy-sensitive content.

Modern photo picker

Android 15 continues refining the secure and streamlined photo picker introduced in earlier versions, offering users better privacy while giving your app access to media in a consistent way across devices.

And of course, there are under-the-hood improvements: better battery life, faster app launch times, and tighter integration with Material You, Google's design language that personalizes your app to match the user's device theme, wallpaper, and style.

Tools of the Trade: Android Studio, ADB, and Emulator

Before you start building apps, you'll need to set up your development environment. This is where you'll write, test, and run your code. Android provides a world-class set of tools that make the process efficient, visual, and even a bit fun.

Android Studio

This is your command center. Android Studio is the official integrated development environment (IDE) for Android development. It's based on JetBrains' IntelliJ IDEA and comes packed with features like a smart code editor, layout visualizers, debugging tools, performance profilers, and built-in support for Jetpack Compose. Android Studio makes coding faster and more intuitive with its suggestions, previews, and real-time feedback.

ADB (Android Debug Bridge)

Think of ADB as your communication line between your computer and your Android device or emulator. It lets you install apps, log information, and control a device through the command line. It's incredibly powerful and helps with testing, debugging, and deploying apps.

Android Emulator

If you don't have an Android phone or tablet at hand, don't worry. The Android Emulator allows you to run virtual Android devices on your computer. You can simulate calls, texts, GPS, sensors, different screen sizes—even battery levels. It's perfect for testing apps across many configurations without needing a physical device.

Together, these tools give you everything you need to create, test, and ship high-quality apps.

Understanding Android Ecosystem: SDK, API Levels, and Releases

The Android ecosystem can be a bit confusing when you're new, but once you get the hang of it, it all makes sense—and it's essential to understand if you want your app to run well across many devices.

SDK (Software Development Kit)

The Android SDK is a collection of software development tools and libraries you use to build Android apps. It includes APIs, documentation, emulator images, and other tools. When you install Android Studio, you're also installing the SDK, which gets updated over time to support new Android versions and features.

API Levels

Every Android version is assigned an API level, which helps developers manage compatibility. For example, Android 15 is API level 35. When you build an app, you'll choose a **minimum SDK version** (the lowest version your app supports) and a **target SDK version** (the version your app is optimized for). This allows your app to work across old and new devices while taking advantage of the latest features.

Releases

Android follows a yearly release cycle. Developers get access to preview versions months in advance to test their apps and adopt new features early. These versions go through developer previews, betas, and finally, a stable release. Google also provides release notes, migration guides, and sample code to make adoption as smooth as possible.

Understanding SDKs, API levels, and the release process helps you future-proof your app, ensure backward compatibility, and make the most of the latest innovations.

This is just the beginning of your Android journey. As you move forward, you'll explore how to design beautiful user interfaces, work with data, handle user input, and build full-featured apps that can live proudly on the Play Store. The possibilities are limitless—and the tools are right at your fingertips. Let's build something amazing.

Setting Up Your Development Environment

Before you can build your first Android app, you need a solid foundation—your development environment. Think of it like setting up your workshop before crafting your first masterpiece. You want everything organized, up-to-date, and working smoothly. Luckily, Google makes this process pretty straightforward, and with just a little guidance, you'll be ready to bring your ideas to life.

Installing Android Studio

Android Studio is your all-in-one tool for Android development. It's where you'll write your code, design your user interfaces, test your app, and prepare it for release. It's built on IntelliJ IDEA and comes with everything you need to get started.

To install Android Studio

Go to the official Android Studio download page on the Android Developers website
Choose your operating system: Windows, macOS, or Linux
Download the installer and follow the setup instructions

During installation, Android Studio will prompt you to install additional components like the Android SDK, SDK Manager, Emulator, and a default virtual device. It's highly recommended to go with the standard setup unless you know exactly what you're doing.

After installation is complete, open Android Studio and give it a minute to configure itself. It may download some additional files the first time you launch it. This is normal—just let it do its thing.

You'll also want to ensure your system has the minimum recommended hardware

At least 8 GB RAM (16 GB is better for emulation and multitasking)
A modern processor with virtualization enabled in BIOS (Intel VT-x or AMD-V)
A solid-state drive (SSD) for faster build and emulator speeds

Once everything is set up, you'll be greeted by the Android Studio Welcome screen. From here, you can create a new project, open an existing one, or explore various tutorials and samples provided by Google.

Configuring the Android Emulator

The Android Emulator allows you to test your app on a virtual device that behaves just like a real phone or tablet. It's incredibly useful when you want to see how your app works across different screen sizes, Android versions, or hardware profiles.

Here's how to configure it

From the Android Studio Welcome screen, click on "More Actions" and select "AVD Manager"

AVD stands for Android Virtual Device

Click "Create Virtual Device" to start the process

Choose a device profile such as Pixel 7, Pixel Fold, or a tablet

Select a system image (like Android 15 - API Level 35)

Download it if needed

Give your emulator a name and adjust settings if desired

Click "Finish" to create it

Once created, your virtual device will appear in the list. You can start it by clicking the green play button. The emulator might take a minute or two to launch, especially the first time, but once it's up, you'll have a fully functional Android device running right on your desktop.

Pro tip

Enable hardware acceleration in your BIOS and ensure virtualization is turned on. This significantly boosts emulator performance.

Also, if you have a physical Android phone, you can use it for testing by enabling Developer Options and USB Debugging. Sometimes testing on a real device helps catch things that the emulator might miss.

Creating Your First Android Project

Now the exciting part—creating your very first Android project. This is where your learning becomes real. Let's walk through the process together.

From the Android Studio Welcome screen, click "New Project"

Choose a template that suits your needs

For beginners, "Empty Activity" or "Empty Compose Activity" is a great choice

Click "Next"

Now enter the project details

Name

This will be the name of your app (e.g., "MyFirstApp")

Package name

This is your app's unique identifier (like com.yourname.myfirstapp)

Save location

Pick a folder on your computer

Language

Select Kotlin (recommended)

Minimum SDK

Choose the lowest version of Android your app should support

Android 8.0 or higher is a good starting point

Click "Finish" and let Android Studio generate the project. It might take a minute or two, but soon you'll see a fully structured project with files and folders laid out.

Your first app will include a basic screen and some starter code. If you chose the Empty Compose Activity, you'll see a simple "Hello Android" displayed using Jetpack Compose.

Go ahead and press the green "Run" button in the toolbar
Select your emulator or connected device
Android Studio will build and launch the app for you

Congratulations! You just created and ran your first Android app.

Exploring Project Structure and Files

When your project is loaded, the structure might look intimidating at first—but don't worry. It's like a toolbox: once you know where everything is, it all makes sense.

Let's explore the main parts of your project

app
This is the main module of your app. It contains all your code, resources, and configuration files.

manifests
Inside this folder is AndroidManifest.xml

This file declares essential information about your app, like its name, icon, permissions, and main activity.

java

This folder holds your Kotlin or Java code. You'll find your activities, composables, ViewModels, and other logic here.

res

Short for "resources," this folder contains everything your app needs to look and feel great

Drawable

Images and graphics

Layout

XML or Compose UI definitions (if not using Compose entirely)

Values

Strings, colors, themes, and dimensions

Raw

Custom media or asset files

build.gradle

There are two of these files: one for the entire project and one for the app module

These control your dependencies, compile options, and other build settings

You'll often come here to add Jetpack libraries or adjust SDK versions

gradle.properties and settings.gradle

These files help configure the build system but can usually be left as-is when starting out

You'll also see the Android view and Project view options in the top-left pane. The Android view simplifies the file structure to what developers care about most, while the Project view shows everything in raw folder format. Feel free to switch between the two as needed.

Over time, as your app grows, you'll become more familiar with how everything fits together. Don't rush it. Every great developer once stared at these same folders and wondered what it all meant. The secret is to keep building and learning, one small app at a time.

Now that your development environment is set up, you've launched your first project, and you've taken a tour through the structure of an Android app—you're ready to start exploring what makes Android truly powerful. Whether it's designing beautiful user interfaces or making your app react to the user in real-time, everything you do from here will build on this foundation.

Take a deep breath. You're not just learning how to code—you're creating tools that could help, inspire, or entertain people all over the world. Let's keep going.

Kotlin Basics for Android

Learning to build Android apps today means learning Kotlin. It's the language Google officially recommends, and for good reason. Kotlin is modern, expressive, concise, and built to reduce the frustration that often comes with coding. If you're just starting out, learning Kotlin will not only make your journey smoother—it'll also give you a major edge in today's Android development world.

Why Kotlin A Quick Overview

Let's start with the big question—why Kotlin

Kotlin is a modern, statically typed programming language developed by JetBrains, the same company behind IntelliJ IDEA, which powers Android Studio. In 2017, Google announced official support for Kotlin on Android, and in 2019, it went a step further and made Kotlin the preferred language for Android development.

Here's why developers love Kotlin

It's concise
You can do more with fewer lines of code. This means less boilerplate, fewer bugs, and easier-to-read code.

It's safe

Kotlin's null safety system helps you avoid the infamous NullPointerException that often crashes Java apps.

It's fully interoperable with Java

You can use Kotlin in existing Java projects and call Java code directly from Kotlin and vice versa.

It's expressive

With modern features like lambda expressions, extension functions, and smart casts, your code becomes clearer and easier to understand.

It's actively maintained and open source

Kotlin evolves quickly to support developers' needs, and the community around it is strong and supportive.

Bottom line

If you're learning Android today, learning Kotlin is the best investment of your time. You'll enjoy writing code more, and your apps will be more stable and future-ready.

Variables Functions and Classes

Kotlin, like any language, is built on core concepts—variables, functions, and classes. Let's explore each of these with simple, easy-to-understand examples.

Variables

In Kotlin, you declare variables using either val or var

val is for values that don't change
Think of it like a constant
var is for values that can change
Like a typical variable in other languages

Example

```
val name = "Alex"        // Cannot be changed
var age = 25             // Can be updated
age = 26                 // This is fine
name = "Sam"             // This would cause an error
```

Kotlin infers the type automatically, but you can specify it like this

```
val name String = "Alex"
var age Int = 25
```

Functions

Functions in Kotlin are easy to write and understand. Here's the basic syntax

```
fun greet(name String) {
    println("Hello, $name")
}
```

You can also return a value from a function

```
fun add(a Int, b Int) Int {
    return a + b
}
```

Or make it more concise using Kotlin's expression body

```
fun add(a Int, b Int) = a + b
```

Classes

Kotlin makes working with classes incredibly simple. Here's a basic class

```
class Person(val name String, var age Int) {
    fun sayHello() {
        println("Hi, my name is $name and I'm $age years old")
    }
}
```

You can create an instance and call a method like this

```
val person = Person("Alex", 30)
person.sayHello()
```

Kotlin also supports data classes, which automatically generate useful functions like toString(), equals(), and hashCode()

data class User(val username String, val email String)

Null Safety and Kotlin Extensions

One of Kotlin's greatest features is its built-in null safety. In Java, dealing with null values can be painful and error-prone. Kotlin helps you avoid null pointer exceptions with smart language design.

In Kotlin, variables are non-nullable by default. That means this is fine

val name String = "Alex"

But this would be an error

val name String = null   // Not allowed

If you want a variable to hold null, you must explicitly declare it with a question mark

var name String? = null
name = "Jordan"

Now, to safely access methods or properties on a nullable variable, you can use the safe call operator

```
println(name?.length)     // Won't crash if name is null
```

You can also use the Elvis operator to provide a default value

```
val length = name?.length ?: 0    // If name is null, length will be 0
```

Smart casts make your code safer and cleaner

```
if (name != null) {
    println(name.length)   // Kotlin knows name is not null here
}
```

Kotlin Extensions

Extension functions let you add new functionality to existing classes without modifying their source code. This is incredibly powerful and clean.

For example, you can write an extension function to reverse a string

```
fun String.reverseWords() String {
    return this.split(" ").reversed().joinToString(" ")
}
```

```
val message = "Hello World from Kotlin"
```

```kotlin
println(message.reverseWords())   // Outputs: Kotlin from World Hello
```

Kotlin extensions are widely used in Android to make UI code more readable and expressive. You'll love using them in your apps.

Using Kotlin with Android Studio

Android Studio is fully optimized for Kotlin. When you create a new project, you'll be prompted to choose your programming language. Choose Kotlin, and Android Studio will generate Kotlin-based code automatically.

Here are a few key features that make Android Studio and Kotlin work beautifully together

Code completion
Android Studio understands Kotlin deeply and gives you intelligent suggestions as you type.

Refactoring tools
You can rename variables, move code around, and change method signatures without breaking anything.

Lint checks and inspections
Android Studio warns you about potential errors and offers quick fixes in real-time.

Kotlin to Java conversion

You can even convert existing Java files to Kotlin by clicking Code > Convert Java File to Kotlin File.

Built-in Jetpack Compose support

If you're using Jetpack Compose, Kotlin is required. Android Studio gives you real-time previews and design tools tailored for Compose development.

Debugging and testing

Kotlin works seamlessly with Android Studio's debugger and testing tools, so you can step through your code and catch issues with ease.

As you continue building your app, you'll start to notice how clean and expressive Kotlin makes your code. It helps you focus on solving problems instead of managing boilerplate, and it encourages best practices right out of the gate.

Kotlin is not just a language you learn—it's a tool that transforms the way you think about building apps. It respects your time, empowers your creativity, and makes Android development feel like a joy rather than a chore. As you dive deeper, you'll come to appreciate its elegance, and before long, it'll feel like second nature.

Next, we'll dive into Android app components, where you'll see how Kotlin fits into the bigger picture of building real, interactive mobile experiences. But for now, give yourself a high five—you're learning the modern way, and you're doing great.

Understanding Android App Components

At the heart of every Android app are its components. These are the building blocks that shape how your app behaves, what the user sees, and how different parts of your app communicate with each other. Think of components like actors in a play—each with a specific role, working together to deliver an experience to your user.

By understanding these components, you'll unlock the power to design seamless, intuitive, and fully functional apps. Let's walk through them one by one.

Activities and Fragments

Activities and Fragments are where your app's interface and behavior come to life. They are often the first things users interact with, and they provide the framework for displaying screens and managing user input.

Activities

An Activity represents a single screen in your app. If you're thinking in terms of a typical app flow, each page—like a login screen, home screen, or settings screen—is usually an Activity.

When you launch an app, Android starts with the **MainActivity**

This Activity is declared in your manifest and marked as the entry point

Each Activity has a lifecycle, meaning it responds to events like creation, pausing, resuming, and destruction

This is useful when handling things like saving user input or stopping background tasks

A simple Activity in Kotlin might look like this

```kotlin
class MainActivity : AppCompatActivity() {
    override fun onCreate(savedInstanceState Bundle?) {
        super.onCreate(savedInstanceState)
        setContentView(R.layout.activity_main)
    }
}
```

This function sets the layout for the screen and initializes any UI elements or data the Activity needs

Fragments

Fragments are modular sections of UI that can be combined inside an Activity. You can think of them as mini-activities that are more flexible and reusable.

Fragments are especially useful when

You want to reuse the same UI element in multiple screens

You're designing a tablet layout with multiple panels

You want to separate concerns within an Activity (e.g., top section and bottom section)

Example use

In a news app, you might have a Fragment for the list of headlines and another for the article details. On phones, they show separately. On tablets, they appear side-by-side in one Activity

Fragments have their own lifecycle too, and they live inside Activities

Modern Android apps often use a single-Activity architecture, where Fragments handle most of the navigation. This pattern, combined with Jetpack Navigation, provides a cleaner and more manageable codebase

Views and ViewGroups

Views and ViewGroups are the essential tools for building your app's user interface. Every button, text field, or image you see in an app is a View. ViewGroups are containers that organize these Views into layouts.

Views

A View is a basic UI component

TextView displays text

Button lets the user tap or click

ImageView shows images

EditText allows user input

These are declared in your layout files (XML or Compose) or created programmatically

Example XML

```xml
<TextView
    android:id="@+id/greeting"
    android:layout_width="wrap_content"
    android:layout_height="wrap_content"
    android:text="Hello, world!" />
```

In Jetpack Compose, the equivalent might be

```kotlin
Text(text = "Hello, world!")
```

ViewGroups

A ViewGroup holds multiple Views or other ViewGroups. It's how you organize and arrange things on the screen

Common ViewGroups include

LinearLayout

Arranges Views in a row or column

ConstraintLayout

Provides powerful and flexible positioning based on constraints

FrameLayout

Stacks Views on top of each other

RecyclerView

Efficiently displays lists or grids of items

When you build your app's interface, you'll use ViewGroups to arrange Views into beautiful layouts. Whether you're using XML or Jetpack Compose, the goal is the same—create something your users enjoy interacting with

Intents and Navigation

Intents

An Intent is how components communicate and how you move between screens. It's like a message your app sends when it wants to do something

Start a new screen

Open a web page or dial a number

Send data to another app

Trigger a background service

There are two main types of intents

Explicit intents

Used when you know exactly which component you want to start

```kotlin
val intent = Intent(this, SecondActivity::class.java)
startActivity(intent)
```

Implicit intents

Used when you want the system to handle the request

```kotlin
val intent = Intent(Intent.ACTION_VIEW)
intent.data = Uri.parse("https://www.android.com")
startActivity(intent)
```

Intents can also carry data using extras

```kotlin
intent.putExtra("username", "Alex")
```

You can retrieve it in the next Activity

```kotlin
val username = intent.getStringExtra("username")
```

Navigation

Navigation is the way users move through your app—from screen to screen, or even back and forth between tabs and sections

In modern Android, the Jetpack Navigation component simplifies this process. Instead of manually managing Fragment transactions or back stacks, you define navigation flows in a visual or XML format using a navigation graph

Benefits of Jetpack Navigation

Automatic back stack management

Support for deep linking

UI-safe navigation commands

Shared ViewModels between destinations

Whether you're using Fragments or Jetpack Compose, Navigation makes your app more predictable, testable, and easier to build

Application and Manifest Basics

Your Android app needs a central place where everything is registered and organized. That's the AndroidManifest.xml file

The Manifest tells Android

What your app is called

What icon it should use

Which Activities it contains

What permissions it needs

Which version of Android it targets

What hardware features it requires

Here's a simple Manifest structure

```xml
<manifest package="com.example.myapp">
  <application
    android:label="MyApp"
    android:icon="@mipmap/ic_launcher">

    <activity android:name=".MainActivity">
      <intent-filter>
        <action android:name="android.intent.action.MAIN" />
        <category android:name="android.intent.category.LAUNCHER" />
      </intent-filter>
```

```
      </activity>

   </application>
</manifest>
```

The Application class

You can also create a custom `Application` class if you need to do setup when the app starts—like initializing analytics, dependency injection, or shared resources

```kotlin
class MyApp : Application() {
   override fun onCreate() {
      super.onCreate()
      // Initialization logic here
   }
}
```

You'll declare this in the Manifest
```xml
<application
   android:name=".MyApp"
   ... >
```

This is optional for beginners, but it's good to know as your app grows in complexity

---

Understanding these components is like learning the grammar of Android's language. Activities, Fragments, Views, Intents, and the Manifest all work together to shape how your app feels and behaves. Don't worry if it feels like a lot right now—every developer starts here. With each new screen you build, each layout you design, and each Intent you send, you'll gain confidence and fluency

The key is to keep building, keep breaking things, and keep learning. You've just unlocked a big door—let's walk through it and see what you can create next

Modern UI Development with Jetpack Compose

User interfaces are at the heart of every mobile app They are what people see touch and interact with every single day And with Android 15 the way we build those interfaces has evolved dramatically thanks to Jetpack Compose

Jetpack Compose is Android's modern declarative UI toolkit It's powerful intuitive and built to simplify UI development so you can focus more on design and functionality and less on boilerplate code Gone are the days of struggling with nested XML layouts and adapter classes With Compose what you see is truly what you code

Let's explore this modern UI revolution together

Introduction to Jetpack Compose

Jetpack Compose is a modern toolkit for building native Android UIs using Kotlin Instead of defining your layouts in XML and inflating them in your code Compose lets you write UI directly in Kotlin functions These functions are called composables and they're reactive meaning the UI updates automatically when your data changes

Jetpack Compose was designed to solve common frustrations with traditional Android UI development

- It removes the need for separate layout files
- It encourages reusable modular UI
- It handles UI updates automatically through state management
- It integrates beautifully with Kotlin and Jetpack libraries
- It simplifies complex layouts like lists animations and transitions

Jetpack Compose is also the default for Android Studio's latest design tools giving you powerful real-time previews and intuitive UI editing

With Android 15 Compose continues to get smarter faster and more dynamic especially with new Material 3 components and dynamic color support built inin

Composables and State

Everything in Jetpack Compose starts with composable functions These are regular Kotlin functions annotated with `@Composable` and they describe what the UI should look like

For example

```kotlin
@Composable
fun Greeting(name String) {
    Text(text = "Hello, $name")
}
```

This composable simply displays a text that says "Hello" followed by the name you pass in

You can call this function inside other composables to build up your UI just like building blocks

Composables are lightweight

They can be reused

They can take parameters

They can respond to changes in data through state

State in Compose

State is what drives your UI Your app's data lives in memory and as that data changes Compose automatically re-renders the UI that depends on it This is called reactive programming and it makes your app feel fast and alive

Here's a basic example

```kotlin
@Composable
fun Counter() {
    var count by remember { mutableStateOf(0) }

    Column {
        Text(text = "You clicked $count times")
```

```
    Button(onClick = { count++ }) {
        Text("Click me")
    }
  }
}
```
```

In this example

`remember` keeps the value of `count` across recompositions

`mutableStateOf` creates observable state

Every time you click the button the `count` changes and the UI updates automatically

This simple pattern is incredibly powerful You'll use it for everything from user interactions to real-time data updates

## Layouts and Theming

Compose gives you a completely new way to organize and arrange your UI elements using layout composables

Some common layout composables include

**Column**
```

Stacks children vertically

```kotlin
Column {
    Text("Item 1")
    Text("Item 2")
}
```

Row

Stacks children horizontally

```kotlin
Row {
    Text("Left")
    Text("Right")
}
```

Box

Allows stacking and overlapping of children—great for layering

```kotlin
Box {
    Image(...)
    Text("Overlay", modifier = Modifier.align(Alignment.Center))
}
```

```
```

LazyColumn and LazyRow

Efficiently render scrollable lists like RecyclerView used to do but much simpler

Layouts in Compose are powered by the Modifier system which lets you control size padding alignment click behavior and more in a readable chained format

Example

```kotlin
Text(
    text = "Styled text",
    modifier = Modifier
        .padding(16.dp)
        .background(Color.Gray)
        .fillMaxWidth()
)
```

Theming in Compose

Compose makes theming your app easy and consistent You define a color palette typography and shapes that apply across your whole app This is powered by Material Design and can be customized to match your brand

Your theme lives in a `Theme` file and wraps your app

```kotlin
MyAppTheme {
  Surface {
    Greeting("World")
  }
}
```

This ensures that every text button and surface inherits the theme unless you override it This makes your UI coherent and beautiful with minimal effort

Material 3 and Dynamic Color in Android 15

Material 3 is Google's latest design system for Android apps offering updated visuals improved accessibility and better support for personalization Jetpack Compose fully supports Material 3 through the `material3` library

With Material 3 you get

Modern components like TopAppBar, NavigationBar, ElevatedButton, and Card.

New design tokens for color typography and elevation

Better support for large screens and foldables

Built-in support for dark theme and dynamic color

Dynamic Color in Android 15

Dynamic color is one of the most exciting features of Android 15 It automatically pulls colors from the user's wallpaper and applies them to your app theme giving users a deeply personal and consistent experience across their device

Using dynamic color is simple in Compose Material 3 handles it for you

```kotlin
MaterialTheme(
    colorScheme = dynamicDarkColorScheme(context) // or dynamicLightColorScheme
) {
    // your UI
}
```

This creates a color palette that matches the system and user preferences You don't need to hardcode colors or maintain multiple palettes

Dynamic color adapts to

Light and dark themes
User wallpaper and system settings
Material You design guidelines

It's supported on Android 12 and up and Android 15 makes it even more fluid and adaptive

---

Jetpack Compose is the future of Android UI development It's clean fast modern and fun It takes the pain out of building beautiful layouts and puts the power back in your hands Whether you're building a to-do app a weather dashboard or the next big social platform Compose is the canvas you'll use to bring your ideas to life

And the best part is—you're not just learning a tool You're learning a new mindset for building UIs One that's focused on simplicity elegance and expressiveness

In the next chapter we'll dive into data handling how to load and manage information in your app using ViewModel LiveData and other architecture tools But for now take a breath and enjoy this moment You've just unlocked a whole new way to build apps and it's only going to get more exciting from here.

Working with Data

Every great app is powered by data Whether it's storing user input fetching updates from an API or remembering someone's preferences how you manage and deliver that data can make or break your app's performance and user experience

Modern Android development makes working with data clean scalable and safe thanks to Jetpack libraries Kotlin Coroutines and lifecycle-aware components This chapter gives you a hands-on introduction to the tools you need to keep your app's data flowing smoothly and intelligently

ViewModels and LiveData vs StateFlow

To build responsive and lifecycle-aware apps you need to separate your UI from your business logic That's where **ViewModel** comes in

A ViewModel is a class that holds and manages UI-related data in a lifecycle-conscious way It survives configuration changes like screen rotations and lets your UI observe and react to data without leaking memory

```
class MyViewModel : ViewModel() {
    val name = MutableLiveData<String>()
}
```

In your composable or Activity you observe this LiveData and update the UI accordingly

```
viewModel.name.observe(this) { newName ->
    textView.text = newName
```

}

LiveData

LiveData is lifecycle-aware meaning it only updates observers that are actively in use (like visible Activities and Fragments) It's perfect for older View-based apps and still works well in Compose if you bridge it properly

StateFlow

For a more modern reactive approach Kotlin's **StateFlow** is becoming the preferred choice especially in Compose

```
class MyViewModel : ViewModel() {
    private val _counter = MutableStateFlow(0)
    val counter: StateFlow<Int> = _counter.asStateFlow()

    fun increment() {
        _counter.value += 1
    }
}
```

In Jetpack Compose you collect StateFlow easily using `collectAsState()`

```
@Composable
fun CounterView(viewModel: MyViewModel = viewModel()) {
    val count by viewModel.counter.collectAsState()
    Text(text = "Count: $count")
```

}

LiveData vs StateFlow

LiveData

Lifecycle-aware

Used in traditional XML UI

Easier for beginners but less flexible in Compose

StateFlow

Kotlin-native

More predictable and testable

Preferred in Compose

Built for structured concurrency and coroutines

In summary LiveData is great but StateFlow is the future especially when paired with Compose and Kotlin Coroutines

Room Database with Kotlin Coroutines

For storing structured data like notes user profiles or saved tasks you'll want to use a local database Room is Google's official SQLite abstraction and it makes storing and querying data simple and safe

Room supports Kotlin Coroutines out of the box making database access non-blocking and easy to read

Step 1 Define an Entity

```
@Entity
data class User(
    @PrimaryKey val id Int,
    val name String,
    val email String
)
```

Step 2 Create a DAO (Data Access Object)

```
@Dao
interface UserDao {
    @Query("SELECT * FROM User")
    suspend fun getAll(): List<User>

    @Insert(onConflict = OnConflictStrategy.REPLACE)
    suspend fun insert(user User)
}
```

Step 3 Build the Database

```
@Database(entities = [User::class], version = 1)
abstract class AppDatabase : RoomDatabase() {
    abstract fun userDao(): UserDao
}
```

Initialize the database

```
val db = Room.databaseBuilder(
    context,
    AppDatabase::class.java, "my-database"
).build()
```

Now you can call database methods inside `viewModelScope.launch {}` blocks to keep your UI thread smooth and responsive

```
viewModelScope.launch {
    db.userDao().insert(User(1, "Alex", "alex@email.com"))
}
```

Room is ideal for caching data offline or building features like saved items bookmarks and local profilesprofiles

DataStore for Preferences and Key-Value Storage

If you need to store small amounts of simple data like user preferences app settings or onboarding flags DataStore is your best friend

DataStore is a modern replacement for SharedPreferences It's safe to use with coroutines and supports two types

Preferences   **DataStore**

 For key-value pairs like theme preference or login state

Proto DataStore

For more complex structured data using Protocol Buffers

Preferences DataStore Example

First create a singleton

```
val Context.dataStore by preferencesDataStore(name = "settings")
```

Define a key

```
val DARK_MODE_KEY = booleanPreferencesKey("dark_mode")
```

Write a value

```
suspend fun setDarkMode(enabled Boolean, context Context) {
    context.dataStore.edit { settings ->
        settings[DARK_MODE_KEY] = enabled
    }
}
```

Read a value

```
val isDarkMode = context.dataStore.data
    .map { preferences -> preferences[DARK_MODE_KEY] ?: false }
```

DataStore is perfect for settings toggles remember-me options or first-time-use checks It's asynchronous and type-safe so you can trust it to behave well across app restarts and updates

Introduction to Paging 3

If your app deals with large data sets like product catalogs search results or social feeds loading everything at once would crash the device or kill performance Paging 3 solves this by delivering data in chunks as users scroll

Paging 3 is tightly integrated with Kotlin Coroutines and Flow and works seamlessly with Room Retrofit and Jetpack Compose

Step 1 Create a PagingSource

```
class UserPagingSource : PagingSource<Int, User>() {
    override suspend fun load(params LoadParams<Int>): LoadResult<Int, User> {
        val page = params.key ?: 1
        val users = api.getUsers(page) // or query Room
        return LoadResult.Page(
            data = users,
            prevKey = if (page == 1) null else page - 1,
            nextKey = if (users.isEmpty()) null else page + 1
        )
    }
}
```

Step 2 Setup Pager in ViewModel

```
val pager = Pager(PagingConfig(pageSize = 20)) {
    UserPagingSource()
}.flow.cachedIn(viewModelScope)
```

Step 3 Collect Paging Data in Compose

```
@Composable
fun UserList(viewModel MyViewModel = viewModel()) {
    val users = viewModel.pager.collectAsLazyPagingItems()

    LazyColumn {
        items(users) { user ->
            if (user != null) {
                Text(user.name)
            }
        }
    }
}
```

Paging 3 handles loading more items retrying errors and keeping scroll performance silky smooth It's a must-have for content-heavy apps like e-commerce social media or news

Working with data is where your app becomes truly interactive and useful Whether you're storing preferences fetching remote info or managing large datasets these tools give you structure clarity and performance

You	now	have	a	powerful	toolkit
ViewModels		to	hold	UI	state
LiveData	and	StateFlow	to	observe	changes
Room	to	manage	structured	offline	data
DataStore		for	lightweight		preferences

Paging 3 for large smooth-scrolling datasets

As you build your app always think about how data flows how it updates and how it stays in sync with the UI Mastering this will set you apart as a professional Android developer and open the door to building apps that truly connect with users.

User Interaction and Input

User interaction is the heartbeat of your app Every tap swipe scroll or input is a moment of communication between your user and your app Designing those moments well is what makes your app feel natural responsive and even delightful

In this chapter we'll walk through how Android handles user input how to respond to events and how to build common UI patterns like menus dialogs and lists Whether you're using classic Android views or Jetpack Compose the goal is always the same—make it easy for users to interact with your app

Handling User Input and Events

At the core of all user interaction are input events—things like tapping a button typing into a text field or swiping on the screen Android gives you a rich set of tools to handle those events cleanly and predictably

Buttons and Clicks in Compose

In Jetpack Compose handling clicks is as simple as attaching an `onClick` lambda to a Button or clickable Modifier

```kotlin
Button(onClick = { /* do something */ }) {

    Text("Click Me")

}
```

Want to make an image clickable

```kotlin
Image(

    painter = painterResource(id = R.drawable.icon),

    contentDescription = "Clickable Icon",

    modifier = Modifier.clickable { /* handle click */ }

)
```

Text Input

For text entry you'll use `TextField` or `OutlinedTextField`

```kotlin

var text by remember { mutableStateOf("") }


TextField(

    value = text,

    onValueChange = { text = it },

    label = { Text("Enter your name") }

)

```

The state pattern ensures that every time the user types the UI updates automatically

Gestures

Want to detect swipes long presses or drags Use `Modifier.pointerInput`

```kotlin

Modifier.pointerInput(Unit) {

  detectTapGestures(

    onLongPress = { /* handle long press */ },

    onTap = { /* handle single tap */ }

  )

}

```

You can even track drag and swipe gestures for more advanced UI behavior

Android also supports keyboard input voice commands gamepad events and more but at the heart of it all is the idea that your app responds to what the user does—and does so instantly and smoothly

Menus Toolbars and Bottom Sheets

Menus and toolbars help users navigate and access key features Bottom sheets offer additional context or options without leaving the current screen

TopAppBar in Compose

```kotlin
TopAppBar(

  title = { Text("My App") },

  navigationIcon = {

    IconButton(onClick = { /* open drawer */ }) {

      Icon(Icons.Default.Menu, contentDescription = null)

    }

  },

  actions = {

    IconButton(onClick = { /* show search */ }) {

      Icon(Icons.Default.Search, contentDescription = null)

    }
```

```
        }

    )

    ```
```

The `TopAppBar` is customizable and can include icons menus and more You can even replace it with a `CenterAlignedTopAppBar` for Material 3

Dropdown Menus

Use `DropdownMenu` to show contextual choices when the user taps an icon or button

```kotlin
var expanded by remember { mutableStateOf(false) }


Box {

    IconButton(onClick = { expanded = true }) {

        Icon(Icons.Default.MoreVert, contentDescription = null)

    }
```
```

```kotlin
DropdownMenu(expanded = expanded, onDismissRequest = { expanded = false
}) {

    DropdownMenuItem(onClick = { /* Option 1 */ }) {

        Text("Settings")

    }

    DropdownMenuItem(onClick = { /* Option 2 */ }) {

        Text("Logout")

    }

  }

}
```

Modal Bottom Sheets

Bottom sheets are a great way to show extra content without navigating away Use `ModalBottomSheet` from the Material library

```kotlin
val sheetState = rememberModalBottomSheetState(skipPartiallyExpanded = true)

val scope = rememberCoroutineScope()
```

```
ModalBottomSheet(

    onDismissRequest = { scope.launch { sheetState.hide() } },

    sheetState = sheetState

) {

    Column {

        Text("More options")

        Button(onClick = { /* Do something */ }) {

            Text("Action")

        }

    }

}
```
```

Bottom sheets are commonly used for filters sharing options or item details
```

RecyclerView vs LazyColumn in Compose

RecyclerView has been a staple of Android UI for years It allows you to efficiently render large lists by recycling views But in Jetpack Compose this has been replaced with something even simpler and more powerful—**LazyColumn**

RecyclerView (Classic View-based UI)

To use RecyclerView you need

An XML layout

A ViewHolder class

An Adapter

A LayoutManager

Often even DiffUtil for updates

While powerful it involves a lot of boilerplate

LazyColumn (Jetpack Compose)

LazyColumn does everything RecyclerView does with a fraction of the effort

```kotlin
val items = listOf("Apple", "Banana", "Cherry")

LazyColumn {

    items(items) { item ->

        Text(text = item, modifier = Modifier.padding(16.dp))

    }

}
```

You can add headers footers and separators just as easily

```kotlin
LazyColumn {

    item { Text("Header") }
```

```
    items(items) { item -> Text(item) }

    item { Text("Footer") }

}
```
```

You can also use `LazyRow` for horizontal lists or `LazyVerticalGrid` for grid layouts

In short LazyColumn is the Compose-native way to build lists and should be your go-to choice unless you're working in an XML legacy app

## Dialogs Snackbars and Toasts

Sometimes you need to interrupt the user with a message ask for confirmation or notify them of an action That's where these come in

### Dialogs

Use `AlertDialog` in Compose for confirmation prompts or modal interactions
```

```kotlin
if (showDialog) {

    AlertDialog(

        onDismissRequest = { showDialog = false },

        title = { Text("Delete Item") },

        text = { Text("Are you sure you want to delete this item?") },

        confirmButton = {

            TextButton(onClick = { /* confirm */ }) {

                Text("Yes")

            }

        },

        dismissButton = {

            TextButton(onClick = { showDialog = false }) {

                Text("No")

            }

        }

    )

}
```

```
```

Snackbars

Snackbars offer brief messages at the bottom of the screen perfect for undo options or minor confirmations

```kotlin
val snackbarHostState = remember { SnackbarHostState() }

val scope = rememberCoroutineScope()

LaunchedEffect(Unit) {

  scope.launch {

    snackbarHostState.showSnackbar("Item saved")

  }

}
```

Place this inside your `Scaffold` like so

```kotlin
Scaffold(snackbarHost = { SnackbarHost(snackbarHostState) }) {

    // UI content

}
```

Toasts

Toasts are old-school quick messages that show briefly on the screen

```kotlin
Toast.makeText(context, "Hello there", Toast.LENGTH_SHORT).show()
```

Toasts are simple but not interactive and don't follow the latest Material guidelines
Snackbars are generally preferred today

Your app is more than a set of screens—it's a conversation between your design and your user Understanding how users interact with your UI and how your app responds is a huge step in making the experience not just functional but enjoyable

You've now got the tools to

Handle clicks gestures and text input

Design menus top bars and bottom sheets

Build smart dynamic lists with LazyColumn

Communicate with users using dialogs snackbars and toasts

Navigation and App Architecture

Navigating an app can be tricky especially as the complexity of your app grows But with the right architecture and navigation strategy in place you can make your app flow naturally keep your codebase clean and ensure that users always know where they are and how to get to where they want to go

In this chapter we will explore the fundamentals of app navigation with both the Navigation Component and Compose Navigation We will also dive into app architecture with a focus on the single activity architecture MVVM pattern and Clean Architecture to help you organize your code logically and keep your app's structure robust and scalable

Navigation Component and Compose Navigation

The Android Navigation Component is designed to simplify navigation in an app by reducing boilerplate code and handling fragment transactions and back stack management automatically It also integrates with Jetpack libraries to improve the user experience

In Jetpack Compose however navigation takes a more declarative approach with Compose Navigation which is deeply integrated with the Compose UI toolkit

Navigation Component (XML-based)

When working with the Navigation Component in traditional Android Views the app's navigation structure is defined using a Navigation Graph (XML) which represents the app's navigation paths including actions and destinations

First add the Navigation dependency to your `build.gradle` file

```gradle
dependencies {

    implementation "androidx.navigation:navigation-fragment-ktx:2.4.0"

    implementation "androidx.navigation:navigation-ui-ktx:2.4.0"

}
```

Then, define your navigation graph in an XML file inside the `res/navigation` folder

```xml
<navigation xmlns:android="http://schemas.android.com/apk/res/android"
```

```
    android:id="@+id/nav_graph"

    android:label="app_name">


    <fragment

        android:id="@+id/fragment_home"

        android:name="com.example.app.HomeFragment"

        android:label="Home" >

        <action

            android:id="@+id/action_home_to_details"

            app:destination="@id/fragment_details" />

    </fragment>


    <fragment

        android:id="@+id/fragment_details"

        android:name="com.example.app.DetailsFragment"

        android:label="Details" />

</navigation>

```
```
```

In your activity you can set up the navigation controller and implement navigation actions like this

```kotlin
val navController = findNavController(R.id.nav_host_fragment)

val appBarConfiguration = AppBarConfiguration(navController.graph)

setupActionBarWithNavController(navController, appBarConfiguration)
```

To navigate between destinations use the `navigate` function

```kotlin
findNavController().navigate(R.id.action_home_to_details)
```

The Navigation Component handles the back stack for you so you don't need to manually handle fragment transactions or back navigation

Compose Navigation

With Jetpack Compose navigation is also simplified into a declarative pattern You no longer need to manage separate XML navigation graphs or fragment transactions Instead everything is part of your composable hierarchy

Start by adding the Compose Navigation dependency to your `build.gradle`

```gradle
dependencies {

    implementation "androidx.navigation:navigation-compose:2.4.0"

}
```

Create a `NavHost` to define your navigation graph

```kotlin
@Composable

fun AppNavigation() {

    val navController = rememberNavController()
```

```kotlin
NavHost(navController = navController, startDestination = "home") {

    composable("home") { HomeScreen(navController) }

    composable("details") { DetailsScreen(navController) }

  }

}
```

Inside the composable you use the `navController` to navigate between screens

```kotlin
@Composable

fun HomeScreen(navController: NavHostController) {

  Button(onClick = { navController.navigate("details") }) {

    Text("Go to Details")

  }

}
```

Compose navigation eliminates the need for fragment transactions and simplifies navigating between different screens making it ideal for new apps built entirely with Compose

Single Activity Architecture

The Single Activity Architecture is a modern approach to building Android apps where you manage navigation and UI transitions within one `Activity` This strategy simplifies the app's flow and minimizes the number of `Activity` components making the app more manageable

Instead of switching between multiple activities you use fragments or composables as destinations in the single `Activity`

Benefits of Single Activity Architecture

1. Simplified Back Stack: With one `Activity` you control the entire navigation stack yourself without worrying about fragment transactions or memory leaks between multiple activities

2. Modularization: You can still break up your app into modules (e.g., by feature or domain) without the overhead of managing multiple activities

3. Consistent UI: By using a single activity you can maintain consistent UI elements like toolbars bottom sheets and side navigation across all screens

In a Compose app the Single Activity approach is even easier with Compose Navigation because all the screens are composables managed within a single activity

Example

```kotlin
@Composable

fun MyApp() {

    val navController = rememberNavController()


    NavHost(navController = navController, startDestination = "home") {

        composable("home") { HomeScreen(navController) }

        composable("profile") { ProfileScreen(navController) }

    }

}


@Composable
```

```
fun HomeScreen(navController: NavHostController) {

    Button(onClick = { navController.navigate("profile") }) {

        Text("Go to Profile")

    }

}

```
```

In this setup, you only need one `Activity` which hosts all the composables via navigation

Deep Links and Navigation Graphs

Deep links allow users to directly navigate to specific content within your app For example a user might tap on a link in an email that opens a specific screen in your app without needing to start from the home screen

You can implement deep links in both the Navigation Component and Compose Navigation

Deep Links with Navigation Component
```

Define deep link support in the navigation graph XML by adding the `android:uri` attribute to a destination

```xml
<fragment

    android:id="@+id/fragment_item_detail"

    android:name="com.example.app.ItemDetailFragment"

    android:label="Item Detail">

    <deepLink

        android:id="@+id/deepLinkItem"

        android:uri="exampleapp://item/{itemId}" />

</fragment>
```

Then, in your `Activity` you need to handle the deep link using `NavController`

```kotlin
```

```kotlin
val navController = findNavController(R.id.nav_host_fragment)

val intent = intent

val deepLinkUri = intent.data

deepLinkUri?.let {

    navController.handleDeepLink(intent)

}
```
```

## Deep Links with Compose Navigation

In Jetpack Compose, handling deep links is just as easy You define a deep link in your `NavHost` configuration

```kotlin
NavHost(navController = navController, startDestination = "home") {

    composable("home") { HomeScreen(navController) }

    composable("details/{itemId}") { backStackEntry ->

        val itemId = backStackEntry.arguments?.getString("itemId")
```
```

ItemDetailScreen(itemId)

    }

}

```

Then, to handle the deep link in the `Activity`

```kotlin

navController.handleDeepLink(intent)

```

Deep links make your app easier to discover and navigate directly to important content

MVVM and Clean Architecture Overview
```

App architecture determines how your app is structured and how components interact It plays a crucial role in making your app scalable testable and maintainable The MVVM (Model-View-ViewModel) pattern and Clean Architecture are two commonly used approaches that can help you achieve this

MVVM Pattern

The MVVM pattern separates the UI layer (View) from the business logic layer (Model) and places the logic in a ViewModel that communicates between them

1. Model: Handles the app's data, usually interacting with a repository to retrieve or save data

2. View: The UI layer that displays data to the user

3. ViewModel: Acts as a bridge between the Model and View It holds UI-related data in a lifecycle-aware way and manages the business logic

This architecture makes your app easier to test and scale while ensuring that the UI remains responsive and decoupled from data management

Clean Architecture

Clean Architecture emphasizes separating the code into different layers with clear responsibilities to make the app more modular and maintainable The layers typically include

1. Presentation Layer: Contains the UI and ViewModel

2. Domain Layer: Holds the business logic and use cases

3. Data Layer: Responsible for data fetching, parsing, and persistence

The main goal is to keep each layer independent and focused on its role This approach helps you manage complexity as your app grows and ensures that the app remains testable and maintainable over time

```plaintext

Presentation Layer (View & ViewModel)

    ↓

 Domain Layer (Use Cases)

    ↓

 Data Layer (Repositories & Data Sources)

```

By understanding and implementing solid navigation and architecture patterns in your Android app you ensure that it is both user-friendly and maintainable Navigating seamlessly between screens becomes natural with the Navigation Component or Compose Navigation while a well-structured architecture keeps your app clean and scalable

You've now learned how to implement the Single Activity Architecture build Deep Links and organize your app with MVVM and Clean Architecture. Next, we'll dive into testing your app to ensure that it works reliably across different scenarios

Permissions and Security in Android 15

Security and privacy aren't just buzzwords in Android development—they're at the very core of what makes an app trustworthy and compliant With Android 15 Google has taken further steps to reinforce user control over personal data and improve app isolation Developers are now expected to not only understand permissions but also implement them with empathy toward users' privacy expectations

This chapter covers runtime permissions changes in Android 15 the updated Privacy Sandbox features how to handle secure data storage and authentication and managing background location access using foreground services

Understanding Runtime Permissions

Android uses a permission-based security model Apps must explicitly request permissions to access sensitive features or data like the camera microphone or user location Starting with Android 6.0 (Marshmallow) and continuing through Android 15 users grant permissions at runtime not during installation

Permission Groups and Types

Permissions in Android are grouped into categories such as

- Normal permissions (like internet access) which are granted automatically

- Dangerous permissions (like location and contacts) which require explicit user consent

- Special permissions (like SYSTEM_ALERT_WINDOW) which need to be granted manually in system settings

Requesting Permissions in Android 15

Here's how to request permissions using the modern **Activity Result API**

```kotlin
val requestPermissionLauncher = rememberLauncherForActivityResult(
    contract = ActivityResultContracts.RequestPermission()
) { isGranted: Boolean ->
    if (isGranted) {
        // Permission granted
    } else {
        // Permission denied
```

```
    }

}
```

Trigger the launcher when needed

```kotlin
Button(onClick = {

    requestPermissionLauncher.launch(Manifest.permission.CAMERA)

}) {

    Text("Request Camera Permission")

}
```

Permission Changes in Android 15

Android 15 continues enforcing one-time and foreground-only permissions Users can now more easily revoke permissions from app settings at any time Apps must be prepared to handle permission loss gracefully

A new privacy dashboard also shows users how often permissions are accessed so developers should make sure their app only uses them when absolutely necessary

Privacy Sandbox and SDK Runtime Changes

Android 15 extends Google's Privacy Sandbox initiative which introduces a more private way to deliver personalized ads without giving developers access to individual user data

SDK Runtime

The new SDK Runtime introduced in Android 14 and enhanced in Android 15 isolates third-party SDKs in a separate runtime environment This means SDKs that handle ads analytics or personalization cannot directly access app data unless explicitly allowed

Key points include

- SDKs are sandboxed away from the host app

- Data sharing is controlled and audited

- SDKs are updated independently through Google Play

This helps reduce misuse of user data by third-party libraries and gives users more transparency and control over how their information is handled

Implications for Developers

If your app uses third-party analytics or ad SDKs you may need to update them to be compatible with the new SDK Runtime and ensure they're compliant with the Privacy Sandbox guidelines

You can opt-in through your manifest and declare SDK dependencies explicitly for better control

Secure Storage and Biometric Authentication

Protecting user data is critical and Android 15 provides multiple layers of protection including encrypted storage biometric authentication and key management

Encrypted SharedPreferences and DataStore

To store user data securely use EncryptedSharedPreferences or Encrypted DataStore
Both encrypt keys and values using AES encryption

```kotlin
val masterKey = MasterKey.Builder(context)

    .setKeyScheme(MasterKey.KeyScheme.AES256_GCM)

    .build()


val sharedPreferences = EncryptedSharedPreferences.create(

    context,

    "secure_prefs",

    masterKey,

    EncryptedSharedPreferences.PrefKeyEncryptionScheme.AES256_SIV,

    EncryptedSharedPreferences.PrefValueEncryptionScheme.AES256_GCM

)
```

Biometric Authentication

Biometrics (fingerprint face recognition etc) can be used for authentication via the BiometricPrompt API. This API supports fallback methods like device PIN or pattern and is recommended for modern secure apps

```kotlin
val biometricPrompt = BiometricPrompt(this, executor, object : BiometricPrompt.AuthenticationCallback() {

    override fun onAuthenticationSucceeded(result: BiometricPrompt.AuthenticationResult) {

        // User authenticated

    }

})


val promptInfo = BiometricPrompt.PromptInfo.Builder()

    .setTitle("Authenticate")

    .setSubtitle("Log in using biometrics")

    .setNegativeButtonText("Cancel")

    .build()
```

biometricPrompt.authenticate(promptInfo)

```
```

Android 15 also supports the new **Credential Manager API** which simplifies and secures login flows across devices including support for passkeys and autofill credentials

Background Location and Foreground Services

Accessing location data is highly sensitive and Android 15 enforces strict policies around background location and the use of foreground services

Foreground vs Background Location

Apps must request both foreground and background location permissions explicitly If your app needs to access location while in the background you must first request foreground permission then background

```xml
```

```xml
<uses-permission
android:name="android.permission.ACCESS_FINE_LOCATION" />

<uses-permission
android:name="android.permission.ACCESS_BACKGROUND_LOCATION" />
```

Ask for background location only if necessary and provide a clear explanation to users why it's needed

Foreground Services in Android 15

Android 15 continues to improve how **foreground services** are managed These services are used when your app must continue executing a task (like tracking location or downloading files) even if the app is not visible

To use a foreground service you must show a notification immediately and use the correct foreground service type in your manifest

```xml
<service
    android:name=".LocationService"
```

```
android:foregroundServiceType="location" />
```

Start the service like this

```kotlin
val serviceIntent = Intent(context, LocationService::class.java)

ContextCompat.startForegroundService(context, serviceIntent)
```

You must also show a persistent notification that tells the user what your app is doing in the background

Android 15 continues tightening rules around foreground services Apps that misuse them (for example, running tasks without showing a proper notification) may be killed or blocked from starting services in the background

By carefully managing permissions implementing secure storage using biometric authentication and respecting new privacy policies like the SDK Runtime developers can build apps that are both secure and trusted by users

With Android 15 users are more empowered to control what data they share and developers are given more tools to earn that trust and deliver secure experiences Understanding how to integrate these privacy and security practices into your app is no longer optional—it's essential

Networking and APIs

Networking is the backbone of many modern Android apps enabling them to fetch data from remote servers and deliver dynamic content to users The Android platform provides various tools and libraries to simplify network operations but one of the most popular and effective combinations for API calls involves Retrofit, OkHttp, Coroutines, and Moshi. These tools help developers handle networking efficiently parse data, and ensure security during communication with APIs

In this chapter we will explore the basics of using **Retrofit** and **OkHttp** for networking, perform API calls with **Coroutines**, parse **JSON** data using **Moshi**, and understand the importance of Network Security Configurations in Android 15

Retrofit and OkHttp Basics

What is Retrofit?

Retrofit is a type-safe HTTP client for Android and Java developed by Square It simplifies making network requests by turning REST APIs into Java interfaces Retrofit uses annotations to define the HTTP method and URL parameters making it easy to connect to remote APIs and parse their responses

To use Retrofit in your project first add the necessary dependencies in the `build.gradle` file

```gradle
dependencies {

    implementation "com.squareup.retrofit2:retrofit:2.9.0"

    implementation "com.squareup.retrofit2:converter-moshi:2.9.0"

    implementation "com.squareup.okhttp3:okhttp:4.9.0"

}
```

Setting up Retrofit

To set up Retrofit you need to create an interface that defines the HTTP requests

```kotlin
interface ApiService {

    @GET("users/{user}/repos")

    suspend fun getRepos(@Path("user") user: String): List<Repo>
```

```
}
```

Next, create an instance of Retrofit using a `Retrofit.Builder`

```kotlin
val retrofit = Retrofit.Builder()

    .baseUrl("https://api.github.com/")

    .addConverterFactory(MoshiConverterFactory.create())

    .build()


val apiService = retrofit.create(ApiService::class.java)
```

With this setup, you can now use `apiService` to make network requests

```kotlin
val repos = apiService.getRepos("octocat")
```

```
```

Retrofit supports various converters (like Moshi for JSON) and HTTP methods such as `GET`, `POST`, `PUT`, `DELETE`, and more It automatically parses the response into Kotlin data classes

What is OkHttp?

OkHttp is a low-level HTTP client that Retrofit uses behind the scenes OkHttp handles the actual HTTP requests and responses and provides features such as connection pooling, request caching, and automatic retries

Although Retrofit is often sufficient for making network requests OkHttp provides additional customization options like adding interceptors for logging or handling authentication

For example you can add an interceptor to log network requests

```kotlin
val interceptor = HttpLoggingInterceptor()

interceptor.level = HttpLoggingInterceptor.Level.BODY
```

```kotlin
val client = OkHttpClient.Builder()

    .addInterceptor(interceptor)

    .build()


val retrofit = Retrofit.Builder()

    .baseUrl("https://api.github.com/")

    .client(client)

    .addConverterFactory(MoshiConverterFactory.create())

    .build()
```

OkHttp's `Interceptor` is useful for debugging network calls and handling responses at a low level

Making REST API Calls with Coroutines

Network calls in Android should not be performed on the main thread to avoid blocking the UI thread Instead use **Coroutines** to perform network operations asynchronously

Setting up Coroutines

To work with coroutines in your project you need to add the necessary dependencies to your `build.gradle` file

```gradle
dependencies {
    implementation "org.jetbrains.kotlinx:kotlinx-coroutines-android:1.5.0"
}
```

Coroutines make asynchronous programming simpler by allowing you to write asynchronous code in a sequential manner which makes it easier to understand and maintain

Performing Network Calls with Coroutines

To use coroutines with Retrofit you can define your API service methods as **suspend functions** Retrofit automatically runs the network call in a background thread and allows you to await the response in a non-blocking manner

Here's how you make a network call in a coroutine

```kotlin
lifecycleScope.launch {

    try {

        val repos = apiService.getRepos("octocat")

        // Handle the repos data

    } catch (e: Exception) {

        // Handle errors like network failures

    }

}
```

Using `lifecycleScope.launch` in an activity or fragment ensures that the coroutine is canceled when the lifecycle owner (like an activity or fragment) is destroyed

This makes the network call lifecycle-aware which helps prevent memory leaks

Handling Network Errors

Network operations may fail due to various reasons like no internet connectivity or server errors Retrofit provides error handling using **Response<T>** and **throwable exceptions**

```kotlin
val response = apiService.getRepos("octocat")

if (response.isSuccessful) {

    val repos = response.body()

    // Handle successful response

} else {

    // Handle error response

}
```

Alternatively you can handle exceptions using the `try-catch` block for more granular control over errors

```kotlin
try {

    val repos = apiService.getRepos("octocat")

} catch (e: IOException) {

    // Handle network failure

} catch (e: HttpException) {

    // Handle HTTP error

}
```

JSON Parsing and Moshi

What is Moshi?

Moshi is a modern JSON library for Android and Java developed by Square It is used to convert JSON data into Kotlin data classes and vice versa Moshi is faster and more efficient than other libraries like Gson and is fully compatible with Retrofit through the `converter-moshi` adapter

Setting up Moshi

To use Moshi in your project add the following dependencies

```gradle
dependencies {

    implementation "com.squareup.moshi:moshi:1.12.0"

    implementation "com.squareup.moshi:moshi-kotlin:1.12.0"

}
```

You also need the Moshi converter for Retrofit

```gradle
dependencies {

    implementation "com.squareup.retrofit2:converter-moshi:2.9.0"
```

}

```
```

Parsing JSON with Moshi

Create data classes that represent the JSON structure

```kotlin
data class Repo(

    val name: String,

    val description: String?,

    val language: String?

)
```

Moshi will automatically map the JSON response to the data class fields

Creating a Moshi Instance

Create a Moshi instance with a KotlinJsonAdapterFactory for Kotlin compatibility

```kotlin
val moshi = Moshi.Builder().add(KotlinJsonAdapterFactory()).build()

val jsonAdapter = moshi.adapter(Repo::class.java)
```

Using Moshi with Retrofit

Once Moshi is set up you can use it with Retrofit by adding the `MoshiConverterFactory` to the Retrofit builder

```kotlin
val retrofit = Retrofit.Builder()

    .baseUrl("https://api.github.com/")

    .addConverterFactory(MoshiConverterFactory.create())

    .build()
```

Now Retrofit will use Moshi to automatically convert the JSON responses into Kotlin data classes

Network Security Configurations

Importance of Network Security

Network security is critical for ensuring that your app's communication with servers remains private and protected from man-in-the-middle attacks or other malicious activities Android provides a Network Security Configuration feature starting from Android 9 (Pie) to help developers enforce secure network connections

Setting Up Network Security Configuration

To enforce secure network connections create an XML file called `network_security_config.xml` in the `res/xml` directory

```xml
<network-security-config>

  <domain-config cleartextTrafficPermitted="false">

    <domain includeSubdomains="true">example.com</domain>

  </domain-config>

</network-security-config>
```

This configuration ensures that only secure (HTTPS) traffic is allowed to `example.com` and all other domains will be blocked for cleartext (HTTP) traffic

Validating SSL Certificates

Android 15 further enhances the SSL certificate validation process allowing apps to specify which Certificate Authorities (CAs) they trust By default Android trusts only system-approved CAs but developers can also specify custom ones for more fine-grained control

Enabling Network Security Configurations in the Manifest

To activate the network security configuration in your app reference the configuration file in the `AndroidManifest.xml` file

```xml
<application

   android:networkSecurityConfig="@xml/network_security_config"

   ... >

</application>
```

This will enforce your security policies and ensure your app only communicates over secure channels

Networking and API calls form the backbone of many modern Android apps By using Retrofit and OkHttp in combination with Coroutines for asynchronous operations Moshi for JSON parsing, and proper Network Security Configurations developers can create efficient and secure apps that communicate effectively with remote services Always keep privacy and security in mind while handling sensitive data and ensure that your network requests are reliable and safe.

Working with Media and Sensors

Android devices are equipped with powerful hardware that lets apps interact with cameras microphones sensors and media playback systems Whether you're building a photo-sharing app a fitness tracker or a multimedia player understanding how to work with these components is essential

Android 15 brings enhancements to camera and media APIs better sensor handling and improved system integrations like the new Photo Picker API Let's dive into how to use these capabilities effectively

CameraX and MediaCapture APIs

Capturing photos and videos is a common feature in many modern apps Android 15 makes this process easier and more consistent across devices using the CameraX and MediaCapture AAPIs

Introduction to CameraX

CameraX is a Jetpack library that provides a consistent camera experience across a wide range of Android devices It abstracts away device-specific quirks and lets developers implement camera features with minimal code

Add CameraX to your `build.gradle` dependencies

```gradle
dependencies {

    def camerax_version = "1.3.0"

    implementation "androidx.camera:camera-core:$camerax_version"

    implementation "androidx.camera:camera-camera2:$camerax_version"

    implementation "androidx.camera:camera-lifecycle:$camerax_version"

    implementation "androidx.camera:camera-view:$camerax_version"

}
```

Using CameraX in a Composable

To display the camera preview in a Jetpack Compose layout use `PreviewView` inside an AndroidView wrapper

```kotlin
AndroidView(factory = { context ->

    PreviewView(context).apply {

        val cameraProviderFuture = ProcessCameraProvider.getInstance(context)

        cameraProviderFuture.addListener({

            val cameraProvider = cameraProviderFuture.get()

            val preview = Preview.Builder().build().also {

                it.setSurfaceProvider(this.surfaceProvider)

            }


            val cameraSelector = CameraSelector.DEFAULT_BACK_CAMERA

            cameraProvider.bindToLifecycle(lifecycleOwner, cameraSelector, preview)

        }, ContextCompat.getMainExecutor(context))

    }

})
```

MediaCapture API in Android 15

Android 15 introduces improvements to the MediaCapture API which streamline the process of recording video and capturing images with higher consistency and less boilerplate code

The `MediaStore` remains an essential tool for storing captured media in the user-accessible gallery

```kotlin
val values = ContentValues().apply {

    put(MediaStore.Images.Media.DISPLAY_NAME, "MyPhoto.jpg")

    put(MediaStore.Images.Media.MIME_TYPE, "image/jpeg")

}

val uri =
contentResolver.insert(MediaStore.Images.Media.EXTERNAL_CONTENT_URI,
values)
```

Use the `CameraX ImageCapture` use case to take a photo and write it directly to this URI

Playing Audio and Video

Android provides multiple ways to play media files including the `MediaPlayer`, `ExoPlayer`, and Jetpack Compose's `Media3` integration for more complex needs

Playing Audio with MediaPlayer

`MediaPlayer` is a built-in class for simple audio playback

```kotlin
val mediaPlayer = MediaPlayer.create(context, R.raw.sample_audio)
mediaPlayer.start()
```

Make sure to release the player when you're done to free up resources

```kotlin
mediaPlayer.release()
```

Using ExoPlayer for Advanced Playback

For more advanced playback like streaming audio or video adaptive quality subtitles and DRM protection use **ExoPlayer**

Add the dependency

```gradle
implementation "androidx.media3:media3-exoplayer:1.2.0"
```

Basic setup for video playback

```kotlin
val player = ExoPlayer.Builder(context).build()

val mediaItem = MediaItem.fromUri("https://your-video-url.mp4")

player.setMediaItem(mediaItem)

player.prepare()
```

```
player.play()
```

```
```` ```
```

You can integrate ExoPlayer with Compose using `AndroidView` to show the video surface

## Background Audio and Notification Controls

When playing media in the background use a foreground service with media session support This allows playback control via the notification bar and lock screen controls Android 15 continues to improve media session integration across the system UI

# Sensors and Motion Detection

Sensors provide valuable information about a device's movement position and environment Android devices typically include sensors like accelerometer gyroscope proximity and ambient light

## Using SensorManager

To access sensors use the `SensorManager` and register a listener
```

```kotlin
val sensorManager = getSystemService(Context.SENSOR_SERVICE) as SensorManager

val accelerometer = sensorManager.getDefaultSensor(Sensor.TYPE_ACCELEROMETER)

val sensorEventListener = object : SensorEventListener {

    override fun onSensorChanged(event: SensorEvent) {

        val x = event.values[0]

        val y = event.values[1]

        val z = event.values[2]

        // Process movement data

    }

    override fun onAccuracyChanged(sensor: Sensor?, accuracy: Int) {}

}

sensorManager.registerListener(sensorEventListener, accelerometer, SensorManager.SENSOR_DELAY_NORMAL)
```

```
```

Unregister the listener in `onPause` or `onStop` to prevent battery drain

Motion Detection and Fitness Apps

Use the Step Counter and Step Detector sensors for pedometer apps These are hardware-backed on many devices and consume less battery than raw accelerometer readings

```kotlin
val                         stepSensor                         =
sensorManager.getDefaultSensor(Sensor.TYPE_STEP_COUNTER)
```

Android 15 optimizes sensor usage with better batching and sensor fusion which reduces power usage while improving motion accuracy

Integrating the Photo Picker (Android 15)

One of the major improvements in Android 15 is the system-wide Photo Picker. It provides a privacy-preserving way for users to share media files with apps without granting broad file system access

Advantages of the Photo Picker

- No need for READ_EXTERNAL_STORAGE permission

- Consistent UI experience across all apps

- Scoped access to only selected media

Using the Photo Picker

To use the picker launch an intent using `ActivityResultContracts.PickVisualMedia`

```kotlin
val pickMedia = rememberLauncherForActivityResult(

    contract = ActivityResultContracts.PickVisualMedia()

) { uri ->

    if (uri != null) {
```

```
    // Process selected image or video

  }

}


Button(onClick = {


pickMedia.launch(PickVisualMediaRequest(ActivityResultContracts.PickVisualM
edia.ImageOnly))

}) {

  Text("Pick a Photo")

}

```
```

You can also allow the user to select both images and videos or limit to certain MIME types

Media Access without Storage Permission
```

Android 15 enforces more privacy around media access Apps should now rely on the system picker instead of requesting broad storage permissions This is especially important for apps targeting Android 14 and above where access to the media store is more restricted

Working with media and sensors in Android allows your app to become more interactive immersive and useful Whether you're capturing a photo playing a song tracking motion or selecting an image Android 15 provides powerful APIs that are easy to use and secure when implemented properly By using the right tools and understanding how Android manages hardware and media you can build experiences that feel smooth modern and responsive to your users.

Notifications and Background Tasks

Delivering timely and relevant information to users is a crucial part of Android app development Whether it's a chat message a weather alert or a background task that syncs data notifications and background processing help keep your app useful and responsive

Android 15 builds on a strong foundation with improved background task management better privacy around notification delivery and tighter control over system resources This chapter focuses on tools and best practices to help you stay up-to-date and efficient

Push Notifications with Firebase Cloud Messaging

Firebase Cloud Messaging FCM is the recommended solution for delivering push notifications to Android devices It allows you to send messages to users even when your app is not running

Setting Up FCM

1 Go to the Firebase Console and create a new project

2 Add your Android app's package name and download the `google-services.json` file

3 Add the Firebase dependencies in your `build.gradle` file

```gradle
implementation 'com.google.firebase:firebase-messaging:23.1.1'
```

4 Make sure to apply the Google services plugin

```gradle
apply plugin: 'com.google.gms.google-services'
```

5 Initialize Firebase in your `Application` class if not already done

```kotlin
class MyApp : Application() {
```

```kotlin
    override fun onCreate() {

        super.onCreate()

        FirebaseApp.initializeApp(this)

    }

}
```

Receiving Messages

Create a `FirebaseMessagingService` to handle incoming notifications

```kotlin
class MyFirebaseMessagingService : FirebaseMessagingService() {

    override fun onMessageReceived(remoteMessage: RemoteMessage) {

        remoteMessage.notification?.let {

            showNotification(it.title, it.body)

        }

    }
```

```kotlin
    private fun showNotification(title: String?, message: String?) {

        val builder = NotificationCompat.Builder(this, "default_channel")

            .setSmallIcon(R.drawable.ic_notification)

            .setContentTitle(title)

            .setContentText(message)

            .setPriority(NotificationCompat.PRIORITY_HIGH)


        with(NotificationManagerCompat.from(this)) {

            notify(1, builder.build())

        }

    }

}
```

Make sure to register your service in the `AndroidManifest.xml`

Sending Notifications

You can send test notifications from the Firebase Console or programmatically from your server using the FCM HTTP API

Foreground and Background Services

Services allow your app to perform long-running operations in the background Foreground services are visible to the user and less likely to be killed by the system while background services are more limited especially in newer Android versions

Foreground Services

A foreground service must display a notification so the user is aware it's running

```kotlin
val serviceIntent = Intent(context, MyForegroundService::class.java)

ContextCompat.startForegroundService(context, serviceIntent)
```

Inside your service class

```kotlin
class MyForegroundService : Service() {

    override fun onStartCommand(intent: Intent?, flags: Int, startId: Int): Int {

        val notification = NotificationCompat.Builder(this, "foreground_channel")

            .setContentTitle("Service Running")

            .setContentText("Doing work in the background")

            .setSmallIcon(R.drawable.ic_service)

            .build()


        startForeground(1, notification)


        // Perform background task

        return START_NOT_STICKY

    }


    override fun onBind(intent: Intent?): IBinder? = null
```

```
}
```
```
```

Foreground services are ideal for GPS tracking file uploads and music playback

Background Service Limitations

Starting with Android 8 and reinforced in Android 14 and 15 background services have strict limitations unless your app is in the foreground or has specific exemptions Instead use tools like `WorkManager` or `JobScheduler` for deferred tasks

WorkManager and JobScheduler

For reliable background work that needs to be deferred and persists across app restarts use `WorkManager` It is a part of Android Jetpack and automatically selects the best method (JobScheduler AlarmManager or Firebase JobDispatcher)

Adding WorkManager

```gradle
implementation "androidx.work:work-runtime-ktx:2.9.0"
```

Creating a Worker

```kotlin
class SyncWorker(appContext: Context, workerParams: WorkerParameters)
    : CoroutineWorker(appContext, workerParams) {
    override suspend fun doWork(): Result {
        // Perform long-running task like syncing data
        return Result.success()
    }
}
```

Scheduling the Work

```kotlin
val workRequest = OneTimeWorkRequestBuilder<SyncWorker>().build()
WorkManager.getInstance(context).enqueue(workRequest)
```

You can also use `PeriodicWorkRequestBuilder` for recurring tasks

`JobScheduler` is the system-level alternative for background work but is more complex and better suited for apps that require fine control or target enterprise use cases

Notification Permissions in Android 15

Starting with Android 13 and continuing in Android 15 notification permissions are now opt-in Apps must explicitly request permission from the user to show notifications

Requesting Notification Permission

Add the permission to your `AndroidManifest.xml`

```xml
<uses-permission android:name="android.permission.POST_NOTIFICATIONS"/>
```

Then check and request the permission at runtime

```kotlin
if (ContextCompat.checkSelfPermission(context,
Manifest.permission.POST_NOTIFICATIONS) !=
PackageManager.PERMISSION_GRANTED) {

    ActivityCompat.requestPermissions(activity,
arrayOf(Manifest.permission.POST_NOTIFICATIONS),
NOTIFICATION_REQUEST_CODE)

}
```

If the user denies the request you should respect their choice and avoid prompting again too frequently Android 15 may also temporarily silence apps that misuse notifications

Best Practices for Notifications

- Only send notifications that are timely and useful

- Use appropriate priority and categories

- Provide notification channels and let users control sound vibration and visibility

- Consider quiet times and avoid spamming

Managing background work and notifications is essential to building responsive respectful Android apps Android 15 enhances this ecosystem with more transparent permission handling improved APIs for background work and a more user-friendly approach to notifications By using tools like Firebase Cloud Messaging WorkManager and proper foreground services your app can stay efficient and helpful without draining battery or overwhelming users.

Building Responsive and Adaptive UIs

Android runs on a vast array of devices with different screen sizes aspect ratios resolutions and user preferences From compact phones to large tablets foldables and desktop-like experiences on Chromebooks building a responsive UI is no longer optional — it's essential

With Android 15 Google continues to improve developer tools and introduce design patterns that encourage flexibility adaptability and accessibility This chapter walks you through key concepts and practices to help your UI shine across all devices and user contexts

Supporting Different Screen Sizes

Android supports a wide range of screen sizes categorized into small normal large and extra-large plus density buckets such as ldpi mdpi hdpi xhdpi xxhdpi and xxxhdpi Responsive UI ensures your app looks great and remains usable regardless of screen category

Layout Tools and Techniques

Use `ConstraintLayout LinearLayout` and `Box` (in Compose) to create flexible layouts Avoid fixed dimensions like `dp` and instead rely on relative sizing weights and constraints

Jetpack Compose makes this more intuitive with modifier chains and the use of `Modifier.fillMaxWidth()` or `Modifier.weight(1f)`

Use `WindowSizeClass` from the `androidx.compose.material3.windowsizeclass` library to detect screen size at runtime and adjust UI accordingly

val windowSizeClass = calculateWindowSizeClass(activity = LocalContext.current as Activity)

when (windowSizeClass.widthSizeClass) {

    WindowWidthSizeClass.Compact -> PhoneLayout()

    WindowWidthSizeClass.Medium -> TabletLayout()

    WindowWidthSizeClass.Expanded -> DesktopLayout()

}

Orientation and Aspect Ratio

Always test in portrait and landscape orientations Consider how your layout adapts when the width increases and height decreases For example switch from a single-column view to a multi-pane layout in landscape

Use `res/layout`, `res/layout-land`, and `res/layout-sw600dp` folders to provide alternative resources for different devices

Foldables and Large-Screen Best Practices

Android 15 supports a growing ecosystem of foldable devices with dual screens flexible hinges and dynamic postures Designing for these devices means embracing UI flexibility and continuity

Jetpack WindowManager

Use the `WindowManager` library to detect folding features like hinges and postures

```
val windowLayoutInfoFlow = WindowInfoTracker.getOrCreate(context)

    .windowLayoutInfo(activity)


windowLayoutInfoFlow.collect { layoutInfo ->

    for (feature in layoutInfo.displayFeatures) {

        if (feature is FoldingFeature) {

            val posture = determineDevicePosture(feature)

            // Adapt UI based on posture

        }

    }

}
```

Adaptive Layouts for Foldables

- Use a two-pane layout for books and tablets with hinges

- Avoid placing buttons or input fields directly over the fold

- Let content flow naturally into each segment

- Support seamless transitions when the device unfolds

Jetpack Compose and Foldables

Compose simplifies layout adaptation with conditional rendering and modifier-based positioning You can use `BoxWithConstraints` to react to available width and height dynamically

Dynamic Theming and UI Modes

Modern Android theming is dynamic and user-driven With Material You and Dynamic Color introduced in Android 12 and enhanced in Android 15 your app can adopt the user's wallpaper and theme preferences automatically

Material 3 and Dynamic Color

Jetpack Compose Material 3 enables dynamic theming with a consistent style across typography shapes colors and more

Enable dynamic theming with Compose

MaterialTheme(

```kotlin
    colorScheme = dynamicLightColorScheme(context),

    typography = Typography,

    shapes = Shapes

) {

    // Your composables

}
```

If you want to support both light and dark dynamic color schemes detect the system theme and apply accordingly

```kotlin
val colorScheme = if (isSystemInDarkTheme()) {

    dynamicDarkColorScheme(context)

} else {

    dynamicLightColorScheme(context)

}
```

Night Mode Support

Use `AppCompatDelegate.setDefaultNightMode()` to support system dark mode preferences

```
AppCompatDelegate.setDefaultNightMode(AppCompatDelegate.MODE_NIGHT
_FOLLOW_SYSTEM)
```

Provide alternative resources like `colors-night.xml` and `themes-night.xml` to ensure your UI looks good in all modes

Accessibility and Localization

Accessibility and localization aren't afterthoughts — they are critical components of a truly responsive UI Android 15 builds on existing accessibility features and internationalization capabilities to support a diverse global audience

Accessibility Best Practices

- Use semantic elements and describe UI with `contentDescription` in XML or `Modifier.semantics` in Compose

- Support TalkBack screen readers with properly labeled buttons and icons

- Ensure touch targets are at least 48dp x 48dp

- Provide keyboard navigation for users with external input devices

Example in Compose

Icon(

```
    painter = painterResource(id = R.drawable.ic_star),

    contentDescription = "Favorite"

)
```

Use `Modifier.accessible()` and `Modifier.focusable()` for better control over UI navigation

Font Scaling and High Contrast

Support system-wide font scaling by avoiding fixed text sizes Use `sp` units and avoid clipping by allowing text to wrap

Test with large text and color inversion settings to ensure readability

```
Text(

    text = "Hello World",

    fontSize = 18.sp,

    modifier = Modifier.padding(8.dp)

)
```

Localization and Right-to-Left Support

Use Android's resource system to support multiple languages by adding `values-es`, `values-fr`, etc

```
<string name="greeting">Hello</string>
```

Provide `layout-ldrtl` variants and enable bidirectional layout mirroring with `android:supportsRtl="true"` in the manifest

Use `LocaleListCompat` from AppCompat to dynamically switch languages if your app allows in-app language selection

AppCompatDelegate.setApplicationLocales(LocaleListCompat.forLanguageTags("fr"))

Responsive and adaptive UI design is the foundation of great user experiences in Android 15 It ensures your app feels native fluid and intuitive across devices from phones to tablets to foldables By embracing tools like Jetpack Compose Material 3 WindowManager and internationalization libraries you can craft interfaces that are not only functional but also delightful and accessible to everyone.

Testing and Debugging

Building an Android app isn't just about writing code that compiles It's about creating reliable and user-friendly software that behaves correctly in real-world situations That's where testing and debugging come in

Android Studio provides a powerful suite of tools for finding bugs writing tests and monitoring app performance Android 15 continues to enhance these capabilities making it easier than ever to catch issues early and improve app quality

Logcat Breakpoints and Debugging Tools

Logcat is your real-time console for viewing logs from your app and the system Use it to print out messages trace stack traces and understand how your app behaves at runtime

Using Logcat

Add logs to your code using `Log` for easy tracking

```kotlin

Log.d("MainActivity", "User clicked on the login button")

Log.e("MainActivity", "Error occurred", exception)

```

Log levels include

- `Log.v()` for verbose

- `Log.d()` for debug

- `Log.i()` for info

- `Log.w()` for warning

- `Log.e()` for error

You can filter Logcat by tag package name or log level to focus on relevant messages

Breakpoints and Step Debugging

In Android Studio you can set breakpoints by clicking the left margin next to a line of code Once a breakpoint is hit during execution the debugger pauses the app so you can inspect variables evaluate expressions and step through your code line by line

Key features include

- Step Over executes the next line

- Step Into enters a method

- Step Out finishes the current method

- Watches monitor variable values

- Evaluate Expression lets you test snippets of code on the fly

This is especially helpful when trying to track down complex bugs or unexpected behavior

Unit Testing with JUnit

Unit testing helps you verify that your business logic works as expected It's fast doesn't require a device and focuses on testing small parts of your code like functions or classes

Setting Up JUnit

JUnit is included in most Android projects by default but you can make sure it's added

```gradle
testImplementation 'junit:junit:4.13.2'
```

Writing a Simple Test

Here's a basic test case for a function that adds two numbers

```kotlin
class CalculatorTest {

    @Test
    fun addition_isCorrect() {

        val result = Calculator.add(2, 3)

        assertEquals(5, result)

    }
```

```
}
```
```

Use annotations like

- `@Before` to run setup code

- `@After` to clean up

- `@Test(expected = ...)` to test exceptions

Run tests with the built-in test runner or from the terminal with `./gradlew test`

## Mocking Dependencies

Use libraries like Mockito or MockK to simulate external classes and dependencies

```kotlin
val mockRepo = mock(MyRepository::class.java)

whenever(mockRepo.getUser()).thenReturn(User("Test"))
```
```

This keeps your tests fast and focused

UI Testing with Espresso and Compose Test

UI testing ensures that your app behaves correctly when interacting with the interface It simulates user actions like clicks typing swipes and validates the output

Espresso for View-Based UI

Espresso is the standard tool for traditional Android UI tests

```gradle

androidTestImplementation 'androidx.test.espresso:espresso-core:3.5.1'

```

Basic test example

```kotlin

@Test
```

```kotlin
fun testButtonClick() {

    onView(withId(R.id.loginButton)).perform(click())

    onView(withText("Welcome")).check(matches(isDisplayed()))

}
```
```

You can simulate user behavior with

- `perform(click())`

- `typeText("username")`

- `scrollTo()`

- `swipeLeft()`

And verify UI with

- `check(matches(isDisplayed()))`

- `withText("expected")`

- `withId(R.id.viewId)`

**Compose Testing**
```

For Jetpack Compose apps use the Compose Test library

```gradle
androidTestImplementation "androidx.compose.ui:ui-test-junit4:1.6.0"
```

Write your test like this

```kotlin
@get:Rule
val composeTestRule = createComposeRule()

@Test
fun testComposeButtonClick() {
    composeTestRule.setContent {
        MyScreen()
    }
```

```
composeTestRule.onNodeWithText("Submit").performClick()

composeTestRule.onNodeWithText("Thank you").assertIsDisplayed()

}

```

Use semantic matchers like

- `onNodeWithText()`

- `onNodeWithTag()`

- `assertIsDisplayed()`

- `performTextInput()`

Compose UI tests are fast and reliable because they interact directly with the rendering layer

Using Profiler and Benchmarking Tools

Testing and debugging help ensure correctness but performance matters too Android Studio's profiling tools help you monitor memory usage CPU activity network requests and more

Android Profiler

The Profiler window shows a real-time overview of your app's resource usage

- **CPU Profiler** shows method traces to detect bottlenecks

- **Memory Profiler** helps catch memory leaks and excessive allocations

- **Network Profiler** tracks HTTP requests responses and payloads

- **Energy Profiler** estimates battery impact

You can capture snapshots and inspect timelines to optimize your app's performance

Benchmarking with Jetpack Macrobenchmark

Android 15 encourages performance testing under real-world conditions Use `Macrobenchmark` to measure app startup jank frame rendering and more

Add the dependency

```gradle
androidTestImplementation "androidx.benchmark:benchmark-macro-junit4:1.2.0"
```

```
```

Create a test

```kotlin
@RunWith(AndroidJUnit4::class)

class StartupBenchmark {

  @get:Rule

  val benchmarkRule = MacrobenchmarkRule()


  @Test

  fun startup() = benchmarkRule.measureRepeated(

    packageName = "com.example.myapp",

    metrics = listOf(StartupTimingMetric()),

    iterations = 5,

    setupBlock = {

      pressHome()

    },
```

```
    measureBlock = {

        startActivityAndWait()

    }

  )

}

```
```

Use benchmarking to track app improvements or regressions across versions

Debugging and testing are your secret weapons for building polished Android apps With tools like Logcat breakpoints JUnit Espresso and the Profiler you can catch bugs early build user trust and keep performance tight Android 15 strengthens these practices by offering more insight into performance permission usage and real-time metrics Use them wisely and your app will not only work — it will shine.
```

Publishing Your App

After months or even years of designing coding testing and refining your Android app the time finally comes to release it into the world Publishing your app means making it available to users through distribution platforms such as Google Play and it requires a series of important steps to ensure everything is secure optimized and compliant with Google's policies

Android 15 has further streamlined the publishing experience but it still demands attention to detail and proper preparation Let's walk through each major step to get your app ready for the spotlight

Preparing for Release

Before you publish your app you need to make sure it's production-ready That means verifying functionality polishing the UI improving performance and checking for any crashes or bugs You also need to disable any development-only code like debugging logs or test backdoors

Clean Up and Optimize

- Remove debug logs and development flags

- Obfuscate your code using ProGuard or R8

- Optimize your app's size using Android App Bundles

- Test your app thoroughly in Release mode

Versioning Your App

Each version of your app must have a unique version code and a clear version name

In your `build.gradle` file update these values

```kotlin
defaultConfig {

    versionCode 3

    versionName "1.2.0"

}
```

The version code is an integer that increases with each release The version name is a string visible to users

Review Permissions

Ensure that your app only requests the permissions it truly needs Extra or unnecessary permissions may slow down approval or cause users to uninstall

Creating Signed APKs and App Bundles

Google Play requires your app to be digitally signed This proves that the app was created by you and hasn't been tampered with Signing is mandatory for both APK and Android App Bundle (AAB) formats

Choosing Between APK and AAB

As of August 2021 Google Play requires all new apps to be uploaded as Android App Bundles not APKs AABs allow Play to deliver optimized APKs for each device configuration reducing download size and improving performance

However you can still generate APKs for internal testing and sideloading

Generate a Signed Build

In Android Studio

1 Open Build menu

2 Click on Generate Signed Bundle / APK

3 Choose Android App Bundle or APK

4 Select an existing keystore or create a new one

When creating a new keystore you'll need to set

- Key alias

- Key password

- Validity period (recommended is 25+ years)

- Organizational details

This keystore is important Keep it secure and never lose it Google does not accept unsigned or mismatched updates

Once done Android Studio will generate your signed bundle in the `release` directory

Upload Key vs App Signing Key

With Play App Signing you upload a key to sign your app before it reaches the Play Store Google then re-signs the app with the official key for distribution This allows you to revoke and replace keys if needed

Upload key = used for uploading

App signing key = used by Play to distribute

Play Store Policies and Guidelines

To publish your app you must comply with Google Play's Developer Program Policies These rules ensure apps are safe respectful and legal Ignoring them can result in removal suspension or even permanent banning

Core Policies to Follow

- Data privacy and user data: Be transparent about data collection and usage Include a privacy policy

- Permissions: Only request permissions necessary for core functionality

- Content restrictions: No hate speech violence or adult content unless age-restricted and legal

- Monetization: Clearly disclose in-app purchases and use Google Play Billing

- Target API level: Android 15 apps must target at least Android 13 or higher depending on current Play requirements

Policy Checklists

Before submission make sure to

- Provide a valid privacy policy URL

- Declare data usage in the Play Console

- Add age ratings and content disclosures

- Handle background location requests properly if used

- Avoid using deceptive or misleading app titles icons or screenshots

Staying compliant helps ensure a smooth approval process and long-term success on the platform

Submitting Your App to Google Play

Once your app is signed and policy-compliant it's time to publish it to the world via the Google Play Console

Create a Developer Account

You'll need a Google Developer account which costs a one-time fee (currently $25)

Go to https://play.google.com/console and sign up

Create a New App

1 Open the Play Console

2 Click on Create app

3 Choose language and default settings

4 Enter your app name

5 Choose whether it's an app or a game free or paid

6 Agree to Play policies

Once the app shell is created you'll see the full submission dashboard

Fill in Store Listing

You need to complete the store presence by filling in

- App title

- Short description (max 80 characters)

- Full description (max 4000 characters)

- App category and tags

- Screenshots (phone tablet foldable etc)

- High-res icon and feature graphic

- Promo video (optional but helpful)

These assets help users understand and trust your app So invest time in quality visuals and clear language

Upload App Bundle

Go to the Release section

- Click on Production > Create new release

- Upload your signed `.aab` file

- Add release notes for what's new in this version

- Review any warnings or errors

- Save and review the release

Set Pricing and Distribution

- Choose whether your app is free or paid

- Select the countries and regions where it will be available

- Configure devices and form factors (phones tablets watches etc)

- Opt into managed publishing if you want to manually control release timing

Submit for Review

After you complete all the sections the console will let you roll out the release

Click on Review and Publish and Google will begin the automated and manual review process This can take a few hours to a few days depending on your app and category

You'll get a notification when your app goes live or if it's rejected with detailed feedback

Publishing your app is both a technical and strategic process From creating signed builds to following Play Store policies and crafting an attractive listing Android 15 continues to streamline and enhance the experience With proper preparation you'll be ready to share your work with the world and reach users across millions of Android devices

Maintaining and Updating Your App

Releasing your app is a huge milestone—but it's far from the end of the journey A successful Android app requires ongoing maintenance updates and optimizations to keep up with new devices user expectations and evolving Android features

Android 15 introduces powerful tools to help developers monitor app health deliver updates strategically and improve performance This chapter explores the key strategies and tools to keep your app running smoothly and growing after launch

Crashlytics and Firebase Analytics

Once your app is live monitoring its performance in the real world becomes critical That's where Firebase Crashlytics and Firebase Analytics come in

Crashlytics

Crashlytics is a real-time crash reporting tool that helps you understand what's going wrong in your app and why It provides detailed reports stack traces and insights to prioritize and fix bugs quickly

Key features

- Real-time crash reporting

- Stack traces with line numbers and source files

- User impact metrics (how many users are affected)

- Crash-free user percentage

- Custom logs to track app behavior leading to crashes

Integration is straightforward Just add Firebase to your project via the Firebase console and include the Crashlytics dependency

```gradle
implementation 'com.google.firebase:firebase-crashlytics'
```

Once enabled Crashlytics automatically logs crashes uncaught exceptions and even ANRs (App Not Responding errors) You can also log non-fatal issues manually

```kotlin
FirebaseCrashlytics.getInstance().log("User attempted login with invalid credentials")
```

This allows you to monitor your app's health across real devices in the real world

Firebase Analytics

Firebase Analytics provides insights into user behavior helping you understand what features people use how they navigate your app and where they drop off

Key features

- Event tracking (screen views button taps purchases)

- User demographics and location

- Retention and engagement reports

- Funnels and conversion tracking

- Integration with Google Ads and Crashlytics

You can track both automatic and custom events


```kotlin
val bundle = Bundle()

bundle.putString("item_name", "Book: Android for Beginners")

bundle.putString("item_category", "Books")

firebaseAnalytics.logEvent("purchase", bundle)
```


Analytics and Crashlytics together help you make data-informed decisions about updates and new features

Handling App Updates and Versioning

Delivering updates to your users is essential Whether it's fixing bugs adding features or optimizing performance versioning and update strategy matter

Semantic Versioning

Use clear versioning practices so users and tools can track changes

- Major version for breaking changes (eg 2.0.0)

- Minor version for new features (eg 1.1.0)

- Patch version for bug fixes (eg 1.0.1)

Update these in your `build.gradle` file

```kotlin
defaultConfig {
    versionCode 5
    versionName "1.3.0"
}
```

The `versionCode` must be an incrementing integer for every release It's used internally by the Play Store to determine whether an update is newer

Update Channels

You can manage updates through the Google Play Console

- Internal testing: Limited group of testers

- Closed testing: Larger beta group

- Open testing: Public beta

- Production: Full rollout

Using these channels lets you release updates gradually and catch bugs early before full release

In-App Updates API

The Play Core Library allows you to prompt users to update your app without leaving it

- Flexible update: Download in background

- Immediate update: Blocks usage until updated

```kotlin
val appUpdateManager = AppUpdateManagerFactory.create(context)
```

This improves update adoption and ensures users benefit from the latest features and fixes

Feature Flags and Remote Config

Updating apps doesn't always require a full release With Remote Config and feature flags you can enable or disable features on the fly

Feature Flags

Feature flags allow you to control whether certain functionality is visible or enabled in the app without changing the codebase

This helps with

- A/B testing

- Gradual rollouts

- Disabling broken or unfinished features

- Running experiments safely

Example

```kotlin
if (FeatureManager.isEnabled("new_home_ui")) {

    showNewHomeScreen()

} else {

    showOldHomeScreen()

}
```

Feature flags can be controlled remotely using a backend or Firebase Remote Config

Firebase Remote Config

Remote Config allows you to change values in your app without publishing a new version

- Instantly adjust UI and behavior

- Segment changes by user group region or app version

- Combine with Analytics for personalized experiences

Example setup

```kotlin
val remoteConfig = Firebase.remoteConfig

remoteConfig.setDefaultsAsync(R.xml.remote_config_defaults)

remoteConfig.fetchAndActivate().addOnCompleteListener {

    val welcomeMessage = remoteConfig.getString("welcome_text")

    welcomeTextView.text = welcomeMessage

}
```

```
```

You can use the Firebase console to update parameters in real time

Performance Optimization Tips

Even if your app works well now future Android versions or hardware changes could expose performance bottlenecks Proactively optimize for speed battery efficiency and responsiveness

Monitor Rendering

Use Android Studio's Profiler and Layout Inspector to analyze frame rendering performance Pay attention to dropped frames slow layouts or heavy animations

- Avoid deep nesting of views

- Use `ConstraintLayout` or Compose with lazy components

- Offload intensive work to background threads

Reduce App Size

A smaller app is faster to install and uses less storage

- Use Android App Bundles

- Enable R8 to remove unused code

- Compress images and remove unused resources

- Use vector assets instead of raster images

Optimize Startup Time

Use the Jetpack Macrobenchmark library to measure and improve startup time

- Avoid blocking operations in `onCreate()`

- Use lazy loading for large datasets or images

- Preload lightweight screens

Memory Management

Keep memory usage in check to prevent crashes and slowdowns

- Use `ViewModel` for lifecycle-aware data

- Clear references in Fragments and Activities

- Avoid memory leaks by unbinding listeners and observers

Maintaining and updating your app is essential to building long-term success With tools like Crashlytics Firebase Analytics Remote Config and performance profilers Android 15 gives you powerful control over the entire post-launch lifecycle Use them not just to react to problems but to stay ahead of user needs market shifts and platform updates.

Bonus: Exploring AI ML and Jetpack Features

Android development is evolving rapidly With Android 15 Google is not just refining the platform—they're supercharging it with AI on-device intelligence and powerful Jetpack libraries This chapter introduces you to cutting-edge tools and concepts that can elevate your apps from useful to unforgettable

From real-time face detection and voice recognition to smart image labeling and personalization the possibilities with AI and ML are more accessible than ever thanks to Google's ML Kit and Jetpack integrations Let's dive in

Android ML Kit Overview

ML Kit is Google's machine learning SDK that brings powerful AI capabilities to Android apps without requiring deep machine learning expertise It wraps common ML use cases into easy-to-use APIs and runs either on-device or in the cloud

Key Features of ML Kit

- Text recognition

- Face detection

- Barcode scanning

- Image labeling

- Language identification

- Smart reply suggestions

- Pose detection

- Translation

These tools can help you build apps that are smarter faster and more context-aware For instance a shopping app could use image labeling to auto-tag items A fitness app could track workouts with pose detection And a chat app could offer smart replies just like Gmail

Using ML Kit in Your App

To use ML Kit first add the dependencies in your `build.gradle`

```gradle
implementation 'com.google.mlkit:text-recognition:16.0.0'
```

```
```

Here's an example of recognizing text from a bitmap

```kotlin
val image = InputImage.fromBitmap(bitmap, 0)

val recognizer = TextRecognition.getClient()

recognizer.process(image)

    .addOnSuccessListener { visionText ->

        textView.text = visionText.text

    }

    .addOnFailureListener { e ->

        Log.e("MLKit", "Text recognition failed", e)

    }
```

It's that simple—and it all runs offline in real time

On-Device AI and Generative Features

With Android 15 the platform is embracing a new generation of AI capabilities including on-device large language models enhanced context understanding and generative media tools

Why On-Device AI Matters

Running AI on-device offers key benefits

- Faster response times

- Offline functionality

- Better privacy

- Reduced server costs

Android 15 introduces APIs and hardware enhancements to accelerate on-device inference Using TensorFlow Lite models you can build powerful AI features like voice commands smart filters recommendation engines and even text generation

Generative Media

One of the most exciting frontiers is generative AI This includes AI-generated art music and text You can use custom models or services like Gemini Nano to power these features in Android 15 devices

Example use cases

- AI writing assistants

- Dynamic story generation for games

- Personalized music composition

- Smart photo enhancements

As Google opens more of these tools to developers Android apps will soon be able to generate rich content on the fly tailored to each user

Using TensorFlow Lite

TensorFlow Lite is the go-to library for deploying machine learning models on Android

You can train models using TensorFlow and convert them to `.tflite` format Then integrate them into your Android app for offline prediction

```kotlin
val interpreter = Interpreter(loadModelFile(context, "model.tflite"))

interpreter.run(inputBuffer, outputBuffer)
```

This brings real-time object detection translation and even natural language processing into your apps

Jetpack Libraries You Should Know

Jetpack is a suite of libraries that help developers follow best practices reduce boilerplate and write robust code These libraries evolve with Android and get regular updates to match the latest features

Here are some Jetpack components worth mastering

Jetpack Compose

If you're building modern UIs Compose is the future It's declarative intuitive and built for Android from the ground up Compose makes it easier to build beautiful animations responsive layouts and dynamic content

Navigation

Simplifies navigating between screens especially with Compose-based apps

- Deep link support

- Safe arguments

- Back stack management

- Single Activity architecture

WorkManager

Best tool for handling background tasks that need guaranteed execution Works even after app restarts

- Perfect for syncing data

- Scheduling backups

- Uploading files in the background

Room

Official SQLite abstraction layer

- Easy-to-use DAO interfaces

- Compile-time query checking

- Integration with LiveData and Flow

DataStore

Modern replacement for SharedPreferences

- Asynchronous and safe

- Supports both key-value and typed data

- Plays well with Kotlin coroutines

Hilt

Powerful dependency injection built on top of Dagger

- Simplifies object management

- Works great with ViewModels

- Reduces boilerplate

CameraX

Modern camera API with backward compatibility and easy integration

- Real-time previews

- Image capture and video recording

- ML Kit friendly

With these Jetpack libraries you can drastically improve your development speed and app quality

What's Coming Next in Android Development

The future of Android is intelligent personalized and cross-platform Android 15 is just the beginning Here's a glimpse of what's ahead

Deeper AI Integration

Google is pushing hard to make AI a core part of Android not just an add-on Expect new APIs for personalization conversational AI and predictive user behavior

Ambient Computing

With wearables foldables tablets and Android Auto developers need to build seamless cross-device experiences The future apps will be context-aware and work effortlessly across screen sizes and form factors

Project Mainline and Modular Updates

More components of Android will be updated directly through Google Play allowing for faster security patches and feature delivery Developers will need to stay flexible and test frequently

Kotlin Multiplatform

Kotlin is expanding beyond Android Use it to share code across Android iOS backend and even web apps Write business logic once and reuse it everywhere

AI-Powered IDEs

Android Studio is getting smarter too With AI-assisted code completion refactoring documentation and bug detection your IDE will soon feel like a coding partner

Exploring AI ML and Jetpack features is a great way to future-proof your Android skills Whether you're building a health tracker or a social app or a productivity tool these tools will help you create more intelligent efficient and delightful experiences for users Android 15 is more than a version—it's a launchpad for the next generation of mobile development.

Resources and Next Steps

You've come a long way—from setting up your first project to exploring AI and Jetpack features But Android development is a constantly evolving field and staying curious is the best way to thrive Whether you're aiming for a career in mobile development or planning to build your own app business this chapter provides resources and advice to keep your momentum going

Official Android Documentation and Codelabs

The first place every Android developer should get familiar with is the official documentation from Google It's comprehensive up to date and loaded with practical examples

Android Developer Site

developer.android.com is the go-to hub

- API references for every Android version

- Developer guides for best practices

- Sample projects and templates

- Device and OS compatibility tips

- Jetpack and Compose-specific docs

You'll find everything from how to use CameraX to the latest updates in Android 15's Privacy Sandbox The search function is incredibly useful when you're stuck or looking for specific functionality

Codelabs

Codelabs are hands-on tutorials created by Google that walk you through building specific features or apps

- Perfect for practical learners

- Usually 30 minutes to 1 hour per lab

- Topics range from UI to Machine Learning

- Many are updated regularly with new Android versions

Some excellent beginner-friendly Codelabs include

- Build your first app in Android Studio

- Using Jetpack Compose basics

- Create a Room database

- Add ML Kit text recognition

Codelabs help you learn by doing and the best part is you can work at your own pace

Top Learning Platforms and Communities

Outside of official resources there's a whole world of communities and platforms that support Android developers—from structured courses to helpful forums and YouTube channels

Learning Platforms

- Udacity: Offers free and paid Android development courses including a Google-backed Nanodegree

- Coursera: Great for academic-style courses that cover Android and Kotlin from the ground up

- Udemy: Huge selection of Android courses many updated for the latest versions

- Pluralsight: For intermediate to advanced developers looking to deepen their skillsets

- YouTube: Channels like Coding in Flow Philipp Lackner and Android Developers are goldmines of free content

Choose platforms that suit your learning style Whether you prefer reading watching or coding alongside an instructor there's something for everyone

Developer Communities

Connecting with other developers can make a huge difference in your growth and motivation

- Stack Overflow: Ask questions and find solutions from developers across the globe

- Reddit: Subreddits like r/androiddev are full of insights news and honest discussions

- Medium and Dev.to: Read real stories tutorials and case studies from working Android developers

- GitHub: Follow open-source projects explore code and even contribute

- Discord and Slack groups: Many Android developer communities host active channels for help and networking

Joining these spaces keeps you plugged into trends solves doubts fast and builds confidence through shared learning

Staying Up-to-Date with Android Development

Android changes fast Staying current ensures your skills stay relevant and your apps stay competitive

Follow Official Blogs and Feeds

- Android Developers Blog: Regular updates from Google about new features tools and practices

- Google Play Console Blog: Tips on publishing monetization and user engagement

- Jetpack Compose Release Notes: Learn what's new in every release and how to upgrade

Watch Conferences and Talks

- Google I/O: The biggest Android announcement stage Watch sessions on YouTube or the I/O site

- Droidcon: Community-led Android conferences held around the world

- Android Worldwide: Free virtual meetups connecting developers globally

Practice With Real Projects

Don't wait for the perfect idea Just build

- Clone popular apps to understand architecture

- Build utility tools to practice API integrations

- Enter coding challenges and hackathons

- Maintain a GitHub portfolio for recruiters and clients

Every project adds value to your skills and helps you discover what you're passionate about

Career Paths and Freelance Tips

Once you're comfortable with the basics you might start thinking about making Android development your career There are several paths you can explore

Becoming a Professional Android Developer

Here's what companies often look for

- Solid understanding of Android fundamentals

- Fluency in Kotlin and Jetpack libraries

- Experience with Git version control

- Familiarity with REST APIs and databases

- Knowledge of MVVM and Clean Architecture patterns

- Projects that demonstrate your skills on GitHub

Build a strong LinkedIn profile maintain a portfolio site and consider contributing to open source or writing tech articles

Freelancing and Indie App Development

If you're more entrepreneurial freelancing gives you creative freedom

- Use platforms like Upwork Fiverr or Toptal to find clients

- Build niche apps and publish on Google Play

- Learn basic UI/UX design principles to deliver polished work

- Master app monetization strategies like in-app purchases ads or premium versions

- Communicate clearly with clients and always document your work

Freelancing can be rewarding but requires self-discipline marketing and continual learning

Whether you're aiming to become a professional Android engineer or dreaming of launching your own hit app the key is to keep learning build often and connect with the community Android 15 opens doors to smarter more beautiful apps—and now you have the foundation to walk right through them

The journey doesn't end here It's only just begun Keep building keep exploring and let your curiosity drive the next big idea